SABBATH

AND

JUBILEE

INCARNATION
Jon L. Berquist

SABBATH AND JUBILEE
Richard H. Lowery

SABBATH
AND
JUBILEE

RICHARD H. LOWERY

Chalice Press.
St. Louis, Missouri

Bible quotations marked NRSV are from the *New Revised Standard Version Bible,* copyright 1989, Division of Christian Education of the National Council of Churches of Christ in the United States of America. Used by permission. All rights reserved.

Those quotations marked RSV are from the *Revised Standard Version of the Bible,* copyright 1952 [2nd edition, 1971] by the Division of Christian Education of the National Council of the Churches of Christ in the United States of America. Used by permission. All rights reserved.

Cover design: Elizabeth Wright
Interior design: Elizabeth Wright

This book is printed on acid-free, recycled paper.

Visit Chalice Press on the World Wide Web at
www.chalicepress.com

10 9 8 7 6 5 4 3 2 1   99 00 01 02 03

Library of Congress Cataloging–in–Publication Data

Lowery, R. H. (Richard H.)
    Sabbath and jubilee / Richard H. Lowery.
        p.cm.—(Understanding biblical themes
    ISBN 0-8272-3826-6
    1. Sabbath—Biblical teaching. 2. Jubilee (Judaism) 3. Sociology, Biblical. 4. Economics in the Bible. I. Title. II. Series.
    BS680.S17 L68 2000
    263'.1—dc21
                                                            99-050534
                Printed in the United States of America

for Henri Nouwen,
who worried about my prayer life,
and for Sharon Watkins,
whose life is my healing prayer

CONTENTS

Preface
ix

1 An Ethic of Abundance and Self-restraint
1

2 Households and Kings, Honor and Shame
7

3 Free the Hebrew Slave!
23

4 Release the Debt! Release the Wealth!
37

5 Proclaim Liberty!
57

6 Sabbath and Creation
79

7 Sabbath and Household Hospitality
105

8 Sabbath Made for Humans
123

9 A Modern Spirituality of Sabbath and Jubilee
145

Scripture Index
153

PREFACE

This book has been a very long time coming. Many people have helped me formulate my ideas on sabbath and jubilee and have supported me in various ways through the long process of writing.

First of all, I am grateful for the patient support of my family. My children, Bethany and Chris, gave up an entire summer of television, noisy indoor play, and vigorous, vital telephone conversations so Dad could work in peace and quiet. They are decent, admirable people. And I am proud of them.

My wife, the Reverend Dr. Sharon Watkins, shuffled her pastoral responsibilities to bear a much greater than normal burden of domestic duties and teenage taxi service. She also read the manuscript in progress and offered helpful suggestions for revision. She has, of course, been my dialogue partner on these issues for many years. As an academic theologian who chose to return to parish ministry, Sharon offered an important perspective that strengthened the book as communication to a theologically sophisticated church audience.

My mother's assistance and support were essential to the success of this enterprise, as were my brother Gary's insightful comments, good humor, and helpful encouragement. I am fortunate that my wife's family is supportive, intelligent, and truly enjoyable. I am especially indebted to my father-in-law, Professor Keith Watkins, an insightful dialogue partner whose scholarly example inspires me.

I am blessed with numerous mentors. Lee Humphreys and David Dungan at the University of Tennessee first taught me to love the critical study of scripture and inspired me to teach. Bob Wilson, Brevard Childs, David Lull, and Leander Keck at Yale helped me hone skills of critical exegesis and gave me models of excellence in scholarship and classroom teaching. I also wish to acknowledge the invaluable contribution and steadfast support of my longtime conversation partner, Ron Allen at Christian Theological Seminary.

I am deeply indebted to student and faculty colleagues at Phillips Theological Seminary. I am especially grateful to Dr. Joe Bessler-Northcutt for the Doctor of Ministry course we taught together in

1996 on the theme of sabbath. Joe and the students in that class helped me clarify my thinking. To my great surprise, Joe showed me that my theology, ethics, and politics actually have logical coherence! I am also grateful to the students in the Master of Divinity seminar on sabbath that I taught in spring 1999 at Phillips Theological Seminary. Their insights and questions pushed me to a deeper understanding of sabbath, sabbath year, and jubilee. I have also benefited greatly from the opportunity to work through some of this material with pastors and laypeople at churches and regional and general assemblies, at the Missouri School of Religion, and especially through the Stewardship Institutes for Clergy, sponsored by Christian Church (Disciples of Christ) financial units, regions, and seminaries, which I have helped conduct throughout the country over the last several years. I have also benefited from conversations with theological educators, pastors, and denominational executives through various events sponsored by the Ecumenical Center for Stewardship Studies.

I wish to acknowledge my indebtedness to Professor Moshe Weinfeld's lifetime of stellar scholarship, but particularly his excellent monograph *Social Justice in Ancient Israel.* His painstaking scholarship is foundational to my own views of sabbath year and jubilee and has truly inspiring implications for liturgy and ethics among peoples of biblical faith. I am also indebted to the revolutionary biblical scholarship of Norman Gottwald.

I thank Jon Berquist, Ched Myers, Tex Sample, Keith Watkins, and Sharon Watkins for reading the completed manuscript.

I am most fortunate to have supportive and challenging colleagues in the Southwest Region of the Society of Biblical Literature and the Association for Disciples Theological Discussion. I was assisted in my research by the Junior Scholar Grant awarded me by the Southwest Commission on Religious Studies in 1995–96. I spent part of my sabbatical in 1996–97 researching and writing portions of this book, thanks to my faculty colleagues and the Phillips Theological Seminary Board of Trustees.

I am especially grateful for the ongoing support I am given as a teacher, scholar, and minister by my president, Bill Tabbernee, and my dean, Gary Peluso-Verdend.

My comments on Genesis 1 in this book represent a substantial revision of an article, "Sabbath and Survival: Abundance and Self-

Restraint in a Culture of Excess," published in *Encounter* 54/2 (1993), 143–67.

Finally, I wish to acknowledge the incredible support I have received on this project from Chalice Press. Dr. David P. Polk has rejuvenated the press. Dr. Jon L. Berquist has long impressed me with his skill as a scholar and teacher of the Hebrew Scriptures. But I have been astounded by his competence and kindness as editor. Jon gave me what I needed to get this book finished: a deadline. I missed it, but not by much.

1

AN ETHIC OF ABUNDANCE
AND SELF-RESTRAINT

M any of us are overworked, while others languish in spirit-killing idleness. Goods and services are inadequately distributed, even when overproduced. Meanwhile, the human-life-supporting natural environment suffers the ill effects of reckless production. These crises pose key challenges for theological reflection today. Sabbath and jubilee offer a fresh angle for people of biblical faith to think theologically about spiritual, social, ecological, and economic limitations and possibilities at the millennium's turn. This book examines the biblical sabbath, sabbath year, and jubilee traditions as part of a broader effort to reflect theologically on this moment of challenge, to build a global ethic of economic and environmental justice, and to encourage spiritual practices of personal, social, and ecological care.

Troubled Souls, Troubled Families

Individuals and families today face a spiritual crisis. We are overworked, stressed out, in debt, and chronically neglecting the basic

1

disciplines of spiritual growth and family nurture. The problem is personal, but its causes and effects are more broadly social and economic.

The emerging global economy offers great potential for human survival and fulfillment, but it also poses enormous threats to social and spiritual well-being. The imperatives of global markets demand more work from fewer workers. There is always more to be done than can be done well in the time there is to do it. The mobility of capital and rapidly changing networks of production and distribution increase uncertainty and undermine the stability of families and communities worldwide. On average, parents are working longer hours for less pay than twenty years ago. Their absence, exhaustion, and anxiety about finances take a toll on the family. Children in wealthy nations have more disposable income than ever before and less access to public space and meaningful participation in the life of the community. The ubiquitous logic of consumption drives young and old to perpetual dissatisfaction. Our spirits hunger for wholeness.

Ecology and Economy

Global economic integration poses serious ecological questions already widely discussed in popular culture. Anyone who can read a placemat at McDonald's knows that bulldozing rain forests in the Amazon region has a negative impact on the natural environment in North America. Saturday morning cartoons teach children that blowing sulfur out of smokestacks can kill trees and lakes half a world away. Wal-Mart recycles. Oil companies contribute to Ducks Unlimited. Madison Avenue thinks there is plenty of "green" to be made in "green-conscious" marketing. Increasing numbers of people of all political persuasions are concerned about how human lifestyles are affecting the ecological balance that makes human life possible.

It is less widely understood, however, that economic inequality also threatens the ability of the ecosystem to sustain human life. Unrestrained consumption at the top of the economy turns vast quantities of natural resources into unusable and irretrievable thermal energy, while producing more garbage and other pollution than the natural environment can process in the foreseeable future.

On the underside of the world's economy, international debt wreaks havoc with the social and natural environment. Rural poverty prompts mass migrations into sprawling cities that are not socially and ecologically viable. Unsanitary conditions there breed virulent diseases that are difficult to treat and hard to contain. The poor cut down trees for fuel, shelter, and space to grow crops just ahead of the desert that creeps closer with every felled tree. While wealth, education, and good health care yield low or no population growth in rich nations, population explodes among the industrializing world's poor, to the severe detriment of the natural environment.

Meanwhile, these ecologically taxing processes are exacerbated by national "debt restructuring" plans imposed on poor countries by the International Monetary Fund. These plans require poor debtor nations to cut domestic spending on health care, education, and job training and to devote the lion's share of the national budget to paying off international loans. To attract the "hard currency" necessary to repay their international debt, they are required to turn their economies into "export platforms," replacing more environmentally friendly subsistence agriculture with cash crops. These crops strain the environment and flood international commodities markets, depressing farm incomes worldwide and creating a chronic global farm crisis. Rain forests are cut, pesticides and herbicides drench fields and pollute water tables, and populations soar in the places least able to absorb more people. Maldistribution of the planet's wealth, especially the crushing burden of international debt, is leading to environmental disaster. Gentler, more ecologically sound lifestyles must include a better distribution of wealth and debt relief for poor countries.

Sabbath and Jubilee

Biblical sabbath and jubilee traditions provide a lens by which to focus theological reflection on the spiritual, ecological, and economic challenges that face us in this era of globalizing economy. In its biblical contexts, sabbath protests conditions of scarcity, overwork, and economic inequality that prevailed under Israel's kings and foreign emperors. By celebrating a divinely ordained cosmic order built on natural abundance, self-restraint, and social solidarity, sabbath critiques the oppressive consequences of a royal-imperial system built on tribute, forced state labor, and debt slavery.

In the modern context of globalizing economy, sabbath can serve a similar critical function. As individual alienation increases and a sense of social solidarity declines, as the boundaries of time and place that once defined the world of work disappear into cyberspace, sabbath speaks a word of proportion, limits, social solidarity, and the need for rest, quiet reflection, and nonconsumptive recreation. In the emerging world, sabbath consciousness may be the key to human survival, prosperity, and sanity.

Ancient Origins and Modern Applications

I am convinced that it is not possible at present to reconstruct the earliest history of weekly sabbath observance. Mesopotamian cultures had market days tied to the lunar cycle, but Israel's seventh-day sabbath is unparalleled in the ancient world. It seems to arise in Israel *ex nihilo*. The Bible only deepens the mystery. Most texts that describe seventh-day sabbath observance are exilic and postexilic or are impossible to date. The references to sabbath that might be preexilic connect it with new moon observance, suggesting that sabbath once was a lunar festival of some sort, perhaps a full moon celebration. It is certain that sabbath became an important part of Jewish cultural identity sometime in the postexilic period among those who finally produced and collected the Hebrew Scriptures. But it is not clear whether this postexilic sabbath had anything at all to do with the "sabbath" mentioned in preexilic texts.[1]

It is also unclear how weekly sabbath is related to sabbath year and jubilee. I once believed that sabbath year and jubilee were expansions of sabbath. Sabbath year and jubilee were "sabbath days with an attitude," sabbath writ large. I now think that the historical picture is

---

[1] There is a long history of scholarship on the origin of sabbath. I find Gnana Robinson's 1975 University of Hamburg dissertation most compelling. It was published in English (with numerous untranslated German citations) as *The Origin and Development of the Old Testament Sabbath* (Frankfurt am Main: Peter Lang, 1988). This in-depth form-critical analysis of sabbath texts is not particularly accessible to a nonscholarly audience, but Robinson's argument is convincing that preexilic references to "sabbath" in the Bible are in fact references to a "full moon day," associated with royal power. After the collapse of the Davidic monarchy in 586 B.C.E., sabbath was associated with seventh-day rest and became a celebration of Yahweh's universal sovereignty. The practical import of Robinson's historical reconstruction is that "sabbath" may not have a single meaning in the Bible, and we need to be very careful in our comparisons of different sabbath texts. There is a very interesting scholarly discussion about the evolution of sabbath as a day of worship (usually dated to the Roman era). A convenient introduction to the issues is found in the composite volume *The Sabbath in Jewish and Christian Traditions* (Tamara C. Eskenazi, et al, ed. ; New York: Crossroad, 1991). The Adventist scholar Samuele Bacchiochi's book *From Sabbath to Sunday: A Historical Investigation of the Rise of Sunday Observance in Early Christianity* (Rome: Pontifical Gregorian University Press, 1977) is an important contribution to the debate. Heather McKay's *Sabbath and Synagogue: The Question of Sabbath Worship in Ancient Judaism,* Religions in the Graeco-Roman World, Vol. 122 (Leiden: Brill, 1994) is the most recent major work. McKay argues that sabbath was strictly a household observance that became a day of communal worship no sooner than 200 C.E.

much more complicated. The development first ran in the opposite direction. I suspect that seventh-year debt release gave rise to seventh-day sabbath. Sabbath day, in turn, became the conceptual model for Priestly "sabbath year" and "jubilee," which are rather different than the older seventh-year "release" laws in Deuteronomy 15 and Exodus 21 and 23. A periodic release from debt and its burdensome consequences eventually was celebrated as a weekly cessation of work. Along the lines of Christian Sunday as a "little Easter," biblical sabbath is a "little sabbath year," a "little jubilee." It is an enduring sign in Israel of the social solidarity and economic justice implied in seventh-year debt release.

Today's consumption-based globalizing economy is in many ways vastly different from the agrarian royal economy in which biblical sabbath was born. But the modern economy puts working people in an updated version of the ancient bind: too much work and not enough money. By exploring several biblical sabbath, sabbath year, and jubilee texts with an eye toward social and economic issues, this book aims to bring the healing wisdom and critical challenge of ancient biblical sabbath tradition into conversation with our own stressed-out, overworked, spiritually starving world.

2

HOUSEHOLDS AND KINGS, HONOR AND SHAME

B iblical sabbath, sabbath year, and jubilee traditions are properly understood in the context of the political economy, kingship ideology, and honor-shame culture of the ancient Near East. A strong commitment to social justice and care for the economically vulnerable provides the literary and legal background for sabbath, sabbath year, and jubilee laws. This humanitarian concern has a theocratic rationale. God's royal honor is at stake in Israel's treatment of "the widow, orphan, and resident alien."

Households

Israel's economic system was essentially unchanged through the entire Old Testament period.[1] The society was mostly rural, with only

---

[1] Most of my discussion of households, agriculture, and royal political economy is adapted from my book *The Reforming Kings: Cult and Society in First Temple Judah,* Journal for the Study of the Old Testament Supplement 120 (Sheffield: JSOT Press, 1991). See especially pages 39–61. I highly recommend the volume by Leo G. Perdue, Joseph Blenkinsopp, John J. Collins, and Carol Meyers, *Families in Ancient Israel,* Family, Religion, and Culture (Louisville: Westminster John Knox, 1997). I am especially indebted to the chapters by Carol Meyers ("The Family in Early Israel," 1–47) and Joseph Blenkinsopp ("The Family in First Temple Israel," 48–103).

a few poorly developed urban areas that served primarily as royal administrative and religious centers. The vast majority of people farmed relatively small plots of land handed down through generations as ancestral property. Social life was organized around mostly self-sufficient villages devoted to agriculture, small-cattle herding, and craftwork. Under Davidic monarch or foreign king, Israel's small farmers were the backbone of this agrarian mode of production. They engaged in subsistence agriculture but had to provide sufficient "surplus" and labor to support the extensive royal bureaucracy and its large-scale "public works"—state buildings, military garrisons, military campaigns, roads, water projects, and so on.

The "household" (*bet 'ab*),[2] a compound family including perhaps three generations, was the basic economic unit. Households consisted of a senior family, adult sons and their wives, and unmarried children. Adult daughters left the birth household and joined the households of their husbands.[3] Wealthy households (a tiny portion of the total population) may have included debt slaves, permanent slaves, a family priest, and affiliated resident aliens.

A typical adult Israelite male had a life expectancy of forty years. Infant mortality rates were high, perhaps as high as 50 percent.[4] So women typically had two pregnancies for every one child who reached age five. Since the economic survival of the household depended on the production of able-bodied children, women married immediately after puberty and were pregnant or nursing for a relatively large portion of their adult life. Dangers of childbirth and the heavy physical toll of multiple pregnancies significantly shortened women's average life span. Few survived to menopause. Most lived about thirty years. Few households faced the need to provide long-term care for elderly parents. Also, life was harsh and medical knowledge was limited. Forty-year-old people might well be in poor physical condition.

It is likely that each conjugal unit in the household had two to six members. With three or so houses in the household complex, the typical *bet 'ab* probably consisted of ten to fifteen people. Though

---

[2]The Hebrew term *bet 'ab* literally means "house of the father." The term *bet 'em*, "house of the mother," also appears, though rarely (Gen. 24:28; Ruth 1:8; Song 3:4; 8:4; see also the women-led households of Prov. 9; 14:1; 31:10–31).

[3]But note the surprising comment at the end of the Yahwist's story about the creation of man and woman: "For this reason, a man leaves his father and his mother and clings to his wife" (Gen. 2:24). This verse seems to assume a matrilocal culture, where the husband leaves his household of birth and joins the household of the wife.

[4]Meyers, "Family in Early Israel," in *Families in Ancient Israel,* 19, 28.

intergenerational tensions and sibling rivalry no doubt were common,[5] the household operated as a single economic unit. Economic functions defined the characteristics of the household, roles of family members, and moral codes that bound families and communities together. Geography and climate shaped the economics of households.

Agriculture

Cereals and grains were the staples of the ancient diet, but the hilly topography and dry climate of Palestine combined with the limited technology available to the ancient Israelites to make large-scale grain production impossible in most of the land. Agricultural terracing and the development of sturdier plows around the 1200s B.C.E. allowed Palestinian farmers to move into the highlands and cultivate land that otherwise could not be farmed. Terraces allowed for small-scale production of grain and cereals, but they were particularly well suited to perennial horticultural crops—olives and grapes. These crops required long-term care. It might be several years after the initial planting that edible crops could be harvested—and then only with sustained care. So property ownership was long-term by necessity.

The extraordinarily varied topography and climate of the land also encouraged long-term land tenure. The uneven highland terrain produces irregular wind and rainfall patterns. As a result, widely diverse ecological niches exist in close proximity. Climate, soil, flora, and fauna can change dramatically in fairly small distances. One farm may sit partially in the rain shadow of a hill or mountain and, therefore, receive substantially less rainfall than neighboring farms. Different wind and water erosion patterns may yield very different soil types and land formations. Though agricultural strategies were broadly similar—mixed crops and small cattle—the particulars varied considerably from plot to plot. Growing the optimal mix of crops on one farm might require different techniques and strategies than those required on the farm next door.

Families relied on highly diversified crops for nutritional balance and also as a hedge against natural disaster. A staggered schedule of planting and harvesting ensured a steady food supply through the year and provided limited protection against uncertain rain, crop

---

[5]It is no accident that striking or cursing a father or mother (i.e., the senior male or female in the *bet 'ab*) is presented in some biblical texts as a capital crime (Exod. 21:15, 17; Lev. 20:9; Deut. 21:18–21; cf. Deut. 27:16).

disease, and pestilence. If one crop failed, the family could fall back on other crops harvested at different times. Cereals, grains, olives, figs, and grapes were the core crops, supplemented by legumes, dates, berries, herbs, spices, onions, greens, and other vegetables. Sheep and goats grazed on agriculturally marginal land, extending the productivity of family holdings. They provided wool, milk, and cheese under normal circumstances and could be slaughtered for meat in hard times. Households in the region shared grazing lands.

The clan (*mishpahah*) was a cluster of households centered around a village. Most households in a village shared common ancestry, but the "kinship" of clan families derived more from shared participation in the enterprises of subsistence than from biological affinity. In the clan, households shared labor for common tasks such as building and maintaining terraces, offered mutual assistance when crops failed, and banded together for defense as necessary.[6]

Men's Work and Women's Work

The unusual ecological diversity of the land shaped family structures and rules of property ownership in ancient Israel. All work was "domestic" in the ancient farm family, and every able-bodied person was engaged in household labor virtually every waking hour of every day, but household work was divided by gender. There was some overlap, but men and women had distinct labor roles in the household economy.[7]

To oversimplify only slightly, men's labor was focused on the production of staple crops, and women's labor on the processing of crops and animal products into food and clothing. Women and prepubescent children tended herb and vegetable gardens close to the houses, processed crops for storage, prepared daily food, cared for small children, and engaged in small craftwork necessary for household subsistence. Food processing and craftwork required technical skill and a high degree of manual dexterity. As a result, women's labor knowledge tended to be more technologically sophisticated and transferable to other households.

Men did the work of soil preparation, plowing, and planting, which required specific knowledge of the farm's particular ecology. So

---

[6]See Norman K. Gottwald's discussion in *The Tribes of Yahweh: A Sociology of the Religion of Liberated Israel, 1250–1050 B.C.E.* (Maryknoll, N.Y.: Orbis, 1979), 257–94.

[7]Meyers, "Family in Early Israel," in *Families in Ancient Israel*, 23–41.

property transfer—or more precisely, the intergenerational transfer of agricultural knowledge about specific plots—necessarily occurred through the male lineage. For that reason and because women's labor knowledge was more technologically sophisticated and mobile, the wife normally left her birth family and joined the household of her husband.

Personal Identity and Social Solidarity

Household and clan had a strong sense of solidarity, reinforced by a culture of honor and shame. Individuals were embedded in a living family at the nexus of a horizontal plane (family past and future) and a vertical plane (ancestral property and gods). Those who were cut off from family, land, or god(s) experienced a severe crisis of personal identity.

Personal alienation is seen in its worst case in the biblical character Job. The book introduces the hero as "Job," not "Job, son of…" From the very first verse then, the ancient reader knew that Job, though "blameless and upright," was in serious trouble. Like Malcolm X centuries later, Job is a man without a family past and, therefore, a man without a clearly defined place in the world. Job then loses his sons and daughters and property. As the reader knows and Job suspects, this series of disasters comes with the permission of his own god. Cut off from family past and future, from his landed place, and even from his god, Job's life is utterly ruined. He is a man without personal identity. It is not surprising, then, that he literally begins to melt down. His physical condition begins to mirror his social condition. His skin becomes porous, and he begins to "leak out," to disintegrate into chaos. Job lives the ancient world's worst nightmare: He becomes a completely freestanding individual, a non-person.

The psychosomatic wholeness of individuals depended on a strong sense of solidarity with the family, its property, and its god(s). The survival of the household was the focal point around which the ancient world was organized.

This starting point leads to a very different ethic than one built on modern notions of social contracts between free individuals. So, for example, while modern readers are likely to see deceitful Jacob as the villain and his thick-headed brother Esau as the victim, the ancient readers of Genesis 25:29–34 had a different view, summed up in the narrator's concluding remark: "Thus Esau despised his birthright."[8] Esau flouts the moral code of the ancient family. Trading his birthright for a bowl of soup is not only stupid, it is utterly immoral. In the ancient view, thank God the morally flawed Esau lost the family property to family members who had the will and way to preserve it.

The senior male had primary responsibility for the survival and prosperity of the household. His honor as a householder depended on the welfare of family members and the preservation of family property. When household members went without due protection and care or when ancestral property was lost, the householder was dishonored.

Mutual Support and Care for the Poor

Other households in the clan were honor bound to help vulnerable households, to mitigate their shame, and to help them restore family honor. This obligation grounds biblical laws and prophetic critiques of social sin.

> If there is anyone in need among you, …do not be hardhearted or tight-fisted…Open your hand. Willingly lend enough to meet the need, whatever it may be!…Give liberally!…Since there will never stop being some in the land who are in need, …open your hand to the poor and needy neighbor. (Deut. 15:7–11)[9]

Loans were subsistence loans. Households borrowed because they needed support to survive. Economically secure households were morally obligated to provide loans to neighbors in need. Because it was immoral to profit from another clan household's misfortune, charging interest on a subsistence loan was forbidden—at least ideally.[10] It was immoral to humiliate a debtor or to place healththreatening conditions on the loan. "When you make your neighbor a loan of any kind, you must not go into the house to take the collateral.

---

[8]All scriptural translations are the author's, unless otherwise marked.

[9]This is the passage Jesus apparently cites in Mark 14:7 (cf. Matt. 26:11; John 12:8) when he scolds the men who scold the woman who anointed Jesus with expensive oil: "The poor you will always have with you." Matthew and John unfortunately drop the important follow-up clause in Mark: "and you are able do good for [the poor] whenever you wish!" Mark's more complete and searing rendition is closer to the sense of Deuteronomy.

[10]Deut. 23:19; Exod. 22:25; Lev. 25:35–37; Ezek. 18:8, 13, 17; 22:12.

Wait outside. Let the person to whom you are making the loan bring the collateral out to you" (Deut. 24:10–11). "Do not sleep in the garment that a poor person has given to you as collateral. Give the collateral back by sunset, so your neighbor can sleep in the cloak" (Deut. 24:12–13).[11]

Special protection was given to households that were partly or wholly cut off from patrilineal support. Resident aliens, widows, and fatherless children were especially at risk. Resident aliens lived away from their ancestral land and from the support of their kin group. Widows and fatherless children found themselves in the dangerous position of being unattached to a male householder. By biblical injunction, the widow, orphan, and resident alien must be treated with exceptional care.[12] Thus, a widow's garment may not be taken as collateral for a subsistence loan (Deut. 24:17). The deuteronomists reserve a triennial tithe for the poor (Deut. 14:28–29) and require that they share in harvest festivals (Deut. 16:9–12). Those who exploit the misfortune of the poor or fail to offer them whatever they need to survive are severely condemned.[13] Poor individuals and households had a moral claim on the wealth of more prosperous families, legally expressed in the right of gleaning. Wealthier households had to leave a portion of their harvest for the poor (Lev. 19:9–10; 23:22; Deut. 24:19–21; Ruth 2; cf. Exod. 23:10–11).

Effects of Monarchy on Household Economy

Three royal policies posed a special threat to households: military draft, forced labor, and taxation. Samuel's speech "The King's Way" (1 Sam. 8:11–17), warns that the king "will take your sons and set them in his chariots and on his horses, and they will run before his chariots" (v. 11). Households also had to provide labor for state projects—tending royal fields; producing weapons; building temples, palaces, storage facilities, roads, water works, and military structures; and fortifying administrative cities and military garrisons (vv. 12–13; cf. 1 Kgs. 5:13–18).[14] Conscripts were paid a subsistence wage for state labor (cf. Jer. 22:13–14), but not enough to compensate the

---

[11]Cf. Exod. 22:26–27; Job 22:6; Prov. 20:16; 27:13; Amos 2:8.

[12]Exod. 22:22; Deut. 16:11, 24:19–21; 26:12–13; Job 29:12–17; Pss. 68:5; 94:6; 146:9; Jer. 7:6; 22:3; Ezek. 22:7; Zech. 7:10; Mal. 3:5.

[13]Exod. 22:21–24; Deut. 15:7–11; Job 22:9, 24:3–4, 9, 23; 29:12–17; cf. Job's plea in 31:13–23; Ps. 94:6; Isa. 1:23; Ezek. 22:7; Mal. 3:5.

[14]See my discussion in *Reforming Kings*, 80–88.

household for the lost labor of able-bodied workers. The drain on labor was coupled with a drain on wealth. The king "will take the best of your fields, vineyards, and orchards...he will take a tenth of your field crops and your vineyard crops and give them to his officers and servants" (v. 15), and "he will take a tenth of your flocks" (v. 17).

Households were caught in a royal vise-grip. They had to produce more with less available labor. Agriculture necessarily began to shift toward producing surplus for royal taxes, but that required greater crop specialization, a perilous strategy. Less diversity meant greater vulnerability to drought, blight, and pestilence. Producing crop and labor "surplus" for the monarchy put families at enormous risk. When households failed to produce enough to meet their obligations and still survive, they were forced to borrow from wealthier households. But the royal drain on household wealth and labor left less to go around, and crop specialization for surplus production left every household more vulnerable to the vicissitudes of nature. The mechanisms of mutual support—interest-free loans, gleaning, acts of charity—were insufficient to meet the need.

A system of interest-lending emerged, as vulnerable households were forced to go outside the clan-based system of mutual support and borrow from wealthy households connected to the royal bureaucracy. As Samuel's speech indicates (1 Sam. 8:14), ancient kings confiscated land and made estate grants to royal officials (1 Sam. 22:7; Ezek. 46:16–17). Recipients often were exempted from military and forced labor obligations, as well as certain taxes. Royal officials also received a share of royal tax revenues: The king "will take one-tenth of your grain and your vineyards, and give it to his officers and courtiers" (1 Sam. 8:15). These political perks put royal functionaries in a commanding economic position. They had the money to make the loans.

Interest debt usually was a vicious circle. Needy householders pledged tools, clothing, the labor of household members, the marriage value of daughters, or in extreme cases the ancestral land itself as collateral for loans. Because it was hard to produce enough the next year to pay the king, repay the loan, and still feed the family, one loan led to another. Eventually, debtors lost ancestral property and entered the creditor's household as debt slaves.

The rich got richer and the poor got poorer as households connected to the crown used interest loans to "join house to house, and add field to field" (Isa. 5:8). Whatever its benefits, the royal system put severe strains on many Israelite households and undermined their ability to preserve ancestral property.

Ideology of Kingship: Prosperity for All, Justice for the Poor

It is ironic that ancient kings saw themselves as guarantors of national prosperity and special guardians of the poor—made poor in the first place by royal taxes and forced labor. In official documents and royal religion, the king was celebrated as divinely appointed householder of the nation, guardian of its ancestral property.

The eighth-century Karatepe Inscription, praising King Azitawada of Adana, makes the point with flair:

> With Ba'al's blessing I have become both father and mother to the Adanites, extending their territory from the rising of the sun to its setting. In my time, they enjoyed all the good things of life, full storehouses, and general prosperity…In all my days the storehouses were full, life was good, and the Adanites dwelt without care or fear."[15]

Kilamuwa of Y'dy Sam'al makes similar claims. "To some I was a father. To some I was a mother. To some I was a brother. Him who had never seen the face of a sheep, I made the possessor of a flock. Him who had never seen the face of an ox, I made the possessor of a herd of cattle."[16] An honorable king made the land prosper.

In Israel, the ritual of anointing (1 Sam. 10:1) symbolically connected honorable kingship and national prosperity. Oil, representing the rich bounty of harvest, was poured over the head of the chosen king—a sign of hope that the land would prosper under his leadership. The king is Yahweh's "anointed one" ("messiah"), a living symbol of national blessing (Pss. 21; 45; 48; 72; and Isa. 45:1–17).

---

[15]Victor H. Matthews and Don C. Benjamin, *Old Testament Parallels: Laws and Stories from the Ancient Near East* (New York/Mahwah, N.J.: Paulist Press, 1991). 115–17. The translations of ancient Near Eastern texts I cite will be drawn from four sources:

   1. Matthews and Benjamin's *Old Testament Parallels.*

   2. Ancient Near Eastern Texts Relating to the Old Testament, 3d ed.; ed. James B. Pritchard (Princeton: Princeton University Press, 1969). I will use the standard scholarly abbreviation *ANET.*

   3. Moshe Weinfeld, *Social Justice in Ancient Israel and in the Ancient Near East* (Jerusalem: Magnes, and Minneapolis: Fortress, 1995).

   4. The Code of Hammurabi, trans. L. W. King; published on the WorldWideWeb by the Avalon Project at the Yale Law School). Information obtained on October 6, 1999 from [http://www.yale.edu/lawweb/avalon/hammeau.htm]. I will abbreviate this as Avalon.

[16]*ANET,* 500–501.

The ideal reign is marked by peace and prosperity.[17] In the words of the exilic or postexilic poet of Amos 9 who longs for the day when God "will raise up the fallen booth of David" (v. 11),

> the time is certainly coming, says Yahweh, when the one who plows will overtake the one who reaps, and the treader of grapes the one who sows the seed. The mountains will drip sweet wine, and the hills will wave [with grain]. I will restore the fortunes of my people Israel. They will rebuild the ruined cities and inhabit them. They will plant vineyards and drink their wine, and they will make gardens and eat their fruit. I will plant them on their land, and they will never again be plucked up....(vv. 13–15)

As householders of the nation, kings bore a special responsibility toward the most vulnerable members of society: the poor, the widow, and the orphan. The purpose of Hammurabi's Code was "that the strong might not oppress the weak,"[18] thus ensuring "the well-being of the oppressed."[19] Hammurabi was "shepherd of the oppressed and of the slaves," "who cared for the inhabitants in their need."[20] Ammisaduqa "established equity for all his people."[21] Lipit-Ishtar prepared "a rod for the wicked" and saved "the people from the evil ones," so that "the powerful no longer oppress them."[22] The Sumerian king Urukagina (third millennium B.C.E.) swore a divine oath not to hand over the widow and the orphan to the powerful.[23] Urnamu (2111–2094 B.C.E.) boasts that he protected the interests of the orphan and widow against those of the rich and powerful.[24] The ability and willingness to protect the vulnerable gave the ancient king his bragging rights. Royal honor depended on the well-being of those least able to protect themselves.

This understanding of royal honor is found in Israel as well. The ideal king "will judge the poor with righteousness and arbitrate with equity for the meek of the land" (Isa. 11:4). The throne of the king who judges the poor in truth will be established forever (Prov. 29:14).

---

[17]Isa. 11:1–9; Jer. 23:5–6; 33:14–16; Ps. 72:16; cf. Hos. 2:8–23.
[18]Weinfeld, *Social Justice*, 48.
[19]Avalon, "Preamble."
[20]Ibid.
[21]Weinfeld, *Social Justice*, 51.
[22]Ibid., 64.
[23]Ibid., 49.
[24]Ibid.

Jeremiah contrasts the unrighteous king Jehoiakim with his righteous predecessor Josiah, whose success came because he "advocated the cause of the poor and the needy" (Jer. 22:13–16). Unlike Josiah, Jehoiakim "builds his house by unrighteousness and his upper rooms by injustice." He "makes his neighbors work for nothing, and does not give them their wages" (22:13; cf. Ezek. 45:8b–12).

Psalm 72 is a prayer of support and guidance for the king, possibly spoken at coronation. Its petitions paint a portrait of the ideal king:

> O God, give your justice to a king, and your righteousness to a king's son. Let him judge your people with righteousness and your poor with justice. Let mountains lift up peace for the people, and hills, righteousness. Let him give justice for the poor of the people. Let him save the children of the needy and crush the oppressor. (vv. 1–4)

The just king and his nation will prosper,

> because he delivers the needy when they cry for help and the poor and those who have no one to help them. He has compassion on the weak and needy, and he saves the lives of needy people. He redeems their life from oppression and violence and puts a high premium on their blood. (vv. 12–14)

The king's just and honorable care merits the following benediction for the nation: "Let there be abundance of grain in the land. Let it wave on the mountaintops, its yield like Lebanon. Let the cities blossom like green plants of the earth" (v. 16).

Yahweh as Householder and King

Yahweh often is portrayed as a householder and monarch. In the ancestral and exodus narratives, in the social legislation of Torah and the prophets' calls to justice, Yahweh is portrayed as special advocate of the weak and poor, protector of the widow and orphan. Israel's God acts like an honorable ancient Near Eastern king.

Yahweh's role as divine sovereign was important to the institution of kingship in Israel. The royal authority of the human king derived from the royal authority of the divine king.[25] As God rules

---

[25] 1 Sam. 9:16; 10:1; 2 Sam. 7:1–16; 1 Kgs. 3:7; 8:16, 25; 9:5; 10:9; 11:31–37.

the universe, the king rules the land (Ps. 89:3–37). The Davidic king is Yahweh's "servant"[26] and "son" (2 Sam. 7:14–15; Pss. 2:7; 89:26–27), God's representative on earth. But after the Babylonians brought the Judean monarchy to a violent end in 586 B.C.E. (2 Kgs. 25), it became even more critical for biblical writers to emphasize the sovereign authority of Yahweh.

This was especially true under Persian imperial policy (after 539 B.C.E.), which did not permit even a puppet king to occupy the throne in Jerusalem. Thus, the anonymous author of Isaiah 45 describes the Persian emperor Cyrus as Yahweh's "messiah" (Isa. 45:1), though Cyrus did not worship nor even know about Yahweh (v. 4). The author affirms Yahweh's royal control of history (43:15; 44:6). Yahweh is Israel's "savior" and "redeemer" (43:3; 44:6; 48:17, 20; 49:7; etc.), the royal kinsman who rescues a household in crisis (cf. Lev. 25:25; Ruth 4:1–12), the king who fathers Israel (49:1–2), and the mother who gives them birth (42:14; cf. Ps. 27:10).[27]

> When Israel was a child, I loved him, and out of Egypt I called my son... it was I who taught Ephraim to walk, I took them up in my arms... I led them with cords of human kindness, with bands of love. I was to them like those who lift infants to their cheeks. I bent down to them and fed them. (Hos. 11:1–4)

> As a mother comforts her child, so I will comfort you. (Isa. 66:13)

God as Royal Champion of the Weak and Vulnerable

As divine monarch and householder, Yahweh is especially concerned for the welfare of the weak. Yahweh "sits enthroned forever" and is "a stronghold for the oppressed" (Ps. 9:7–9). God is "king forever and ever," "the helper of the orphan" (Ps. 10:14–16), who does "justice for the orphan and the oppressed" (v. 18). Yahweh defends the poor and needy (Pss. 12:5; 140:12). Under God's dominion, "the poor will eat and be satisfied" (Ps. 22:26, 28) because Yahweh "protects them and keeps them alive" (Ps. 41:1–2). God is "father of

---

[26]2 Sam. 7:5, 8, 19–21, 25–29; 1 Kgs. 3:6–9; 8:23–26.
[27]Cf. Deut. 32:6; Ps. 103:13; Isa. 1:2–4; 63:8, 16; 64:8; Jer. 3:4, 19; 31:9; Mal. 1:6; 2:10.

orphans and protector of widows" (Ps. 68:5). "God gives the desolate a home to live in" and "leads prisoners out to prosperity" (Ps. 68:6). Yahweh "hears the needy, and does not despise his own who are in bondage" (Ps. 69:33). Israel's God demands justice in the divine council: "Give justice to the weak and the orphan! Maintain the right of the lowly and the destitute! Rescue the weak and the needy! Deliver them from the hand of the wicked" (Ps. 82:3–4; cf. 103:6). Yahweh "raises the poor from the dust, and lifts the needy from the ash heap to make them sit with princes" and "gives the barren woman a home, making her the joyous mother of children" (Ps. 113:7–9). Yahweh lifts up the downtrodden (Ps. 147:6) and reigns forever (Ps. 146:10). God executes justice for the oppressed, gives food to the hungry, sets the prisoners free, opens the eyes of the blind, lifts up those who are bowed down, watches over strangers, upholds the orphan and the widow, and brings the way of the wicked to ruin (Ps. 146:7–9).

Hannah's astonishing prayer at the birth of her son Samuel expresses Israel's hope in Yahweh as royal liberator of the oppressed (1 Sam. 2:1–10; cf. Luke 1:46–55).

> My heart rejoices in Yahweh! My strength is lifted up in Yahweh. My mouth ridicules my enemies, because I joy in my salvation: There is no holy one like Yahweh, indeed no one besides you! There is no rock like our God! Do not keep talking so high and mighty—arrogant words coming out of your mouths. Yahweh is a God of knowledge. By him, deeds are measured. The bows of the mighty are shattered. The feeble are girded with strength. The affluent have hired themselves out for food, while the hungry stop being hungry… Yahweh … raises the poor from the dust, lifts the needy from the ash-heap, seating them among princes, giving them a throne of honor as an inheritance. For the pillars of the earth belong to Yahweh. He has set the world on them. (1 Sam. 2:1–8)

God as Giver of Abundant Life

As royal householder of Israel, Yahweh brings prosperity to the people and provides lavish bounty. "Happy are those who fear Yahweh! Their descendants will be mighty in the land… wealth and riches are in their houses" (Ps. 112:1–3). They "will eat the fruit of the labor of [their] hands." Their wives "will be like a fruitful vine," their "children will be like olive shoots around [their] table" (Ps. 128:2–3). Yahweh will "abundantly bless the provisions" of Israel and "satisfy its poor with bread" (Ps. 132:15). God "covers the heavens with clouds, prepares the rain for the earth, makes grass grow on the hills… grants peace within your borders, and fills you with the finest wheat" (Ps. 147:8, 14). God is "the hope of all the ends of the earth" (Ps. 65:5). In the words of the psalmist's song,

> you provide the people with grain… You water its furrows abundantly, settling its ridges, softening it with showers, and blessing its growth. You crown the year with your bounty; your wagon tracks overflow with richness. The pastures of the wilderness overflow, the hills gird themselves with joy, the meadows clothe themselves with flocks, the valleys deck themselves with grain, they shout and sing together for joy. (Ps. 65:9–13)

The people take refuge in the shadow of God's wings. "They feast on the abundance of your house, and you give them drink from the river of your delights. For with you is the fountain of life" (Ps. 36: 7–9).

God is the divine host, providing hospitality and healing care for those in need. "Even though I walk through the valley of death's shadows, I will fear no evil; for you are with me; your rod and your staff—they comfort me. You prepare a table before me in the presence of my enemies; you anoint my head with oil; my cup overflows" (Ps. 23:4–5).

It is not surprising that this God chooses to bless all the nations of the earth (Gen. 12:3) through the lineage of a resident alien, a "wandering Aramean" (Deut. 26:5), or to make a world debut liberating slaves from Egypt.

As royal householder of the nation, Yahweh's honor was at stake in the welfare of the people, particularly the most vulnerable. Social justice in Israel had a theocratic rationale. Fairness, equity, and especially care for the suffering poor were signs of Yahweh's sovereign authority among the people. Injustice and lack of compassion were acts of rebellion, public affronts to God's sovereign power. Thus, Deuteronomy offers this rationale for acts of kindness and mercy: "Remember that you were a slave in the land of Egypt, and Yahweh your God redeemed you!" Leviticus puts the call to justice more simply still: "I am Yahweh!" Social justice and mutual care is right worship, lived allegiance to the sovereign God (Ps. 15; Amos 5:24; Mic. 6:8).

Summary

Agriculture in ancient Palestine was difficult under the best of circumstances. The harsh and highly diverse conditions of the highland environment shaped the contours of agrarian life in Israel. By necessity, multigenerational households were the fundamental economic units, though households tended to group together in clans around small villages. There was a high level of social solidarity within the household and between households in a clan. Individual behavior was directed toward the survival of the family and its property, and households provided mutual support at no charge as needed. Land was held by families over long periods of time, and property passed through the male lineage. The honor of the household and its senior male depended on the well-being of all its family members and the preservation of household property.

Royal tax and labor policies destabilized households, draining family resources and partially shifting production from subsistence toward riskier surplus farming. Households pressured by royal taxes and labor demands increasingly relied on interest loans from wealthy households connected to the crown. The vicious circle of debt often ended in debt slavery and loss of ancestral property.

Though royal policies made farm households more vulnerable, royal ideology cast the king as savior of the weak and defender of the poor. As chief householder of the nation, the king was special protector of those who fell through the cracks of the economy. The king's honor was tied to the welfare of the poor. His success and the nation's prosperity depended on how well he cared for the weak and defended those in trouble.

In the Bible, Yahweh was celebrated as divine monarch, the cosmic father and mother of Israel. Yahweh's reputation as householder and king was tied to the welfare of the people. When the kings and leaders of Israel failed to support the poor and vulnerable, they dishonored themselves and shamed Yahweh. Social justice was a matter of divine honor. Social injustice was blasphemy.

3

FREE THE HEBREW SLAVE!

S abbath-year and jubilee traditions include a variety of actual practices and utopian programs that share a common founda- tion in the household-oriented culture of ancient Israel. These traditions are shaped by the ideology of kingship and especially by the idea that Yahweh is divine monarch of Israel. They are grounded in a strong sense of social solidarity, characteristic of the Bible's social legislation and prophetic critiques of injustice. Sabbath-year and ju- bilee practices go to the very heart of Israel's identity as a people re- deemed by Yahweh from slavery in Egypt. Sabbath year and jubilee are manifestations of God's sovereignty in Israel and the world. This chapter and the next address sabbath year.

Of the three main sabbath-year texts in the Bible (Exod. 23:10– 11; Deut. 15:1–18; and Lev. 25:1–7, 18–24), only the latest one, Leviticus 25, describes the seventh year as "sabbath" year. The sev- enth year is a "sabbath of complete rest (*shabbat shabbatôn*) for the land," a "sabbath for Yahweh," according to Leviticus 25:4. Sabbath year in Leviticus offers a utopian vision closely connected with sabbath- creation in Genesis 1 and sabbath-manna in Exodus 16. Exodus 23 ties the seventh year to the seventh-day sabbath, but without actually

23

calling it a sabbath year (Exod. 23:9–12). Deuteronomy 15:1–18, the most comprehensive seventh-year law, speaks of a debt release for Yahweh. It also expands an ancient law that sets a cap on the length of time a debt slave may serve. The law appears in simpler form in Exodus 21:2.

Exodus 21:2–11

The book of Exodus took its current shape sometime after the Babylonian exile, though it certainly contains material that predates the destruction of Jerusalem in 586 B.C.E. The slave laws in Exodus 21:2–11, 26–27 are in a coherent subsection of Exodus that contains what is generally thought to be the oldest legislation in the Bible. The so-called "Book of the Covenant" (20:22—23:33) includes laws that are similar in form and content to Mesopotamian codes from the nineteenth and eighteenth Centuries B.C.E.,[1] several centuries before the appearance of Israel in Canaan. Though many of the laws in the Book of the Covenant are ancient and not unique to Israel, some, such as the sabbath law (23:12), have no clear parallel in known ancient literature outside of Israel and are difficult to date. Furthermore, the undeniable antiquity of many of the laws does not guarantee that the Book of the Covenant as a whole is particularly old or that every law in it is ancient.

Free Without Debt

> When you acquire a Hebrew slave, he may serve six years, but in the seventh he will go out free, without debt. (Exod. 21:2)

Exodus 21:2 is often discussed among the sabbath-year passages, though it neither uses the term "sabbath" nor envisions a universal emancipation every seven years. It is, rather, Israel's version of a very old Near Eastern law that puts an upper limit on the length of time a debt slave must serve to pay off his debt. This slave-release law and other laws about "Hebrew slaves" in verses 3–11 are similar in form and content to laws about debt slaves in the eighteenth century Babylonian Code of Hammurabi, though the Babylonian law is more generous to the slave:

---

[1] The nineteenth century B.C.E. Laws of Eshnunna (*ANET,* 161–63) and the eighteenth century B.C.E. Code of Hammurabi (*ANET,* 163–64, 166–77) respectively.

If anyone fails to meet a claim for a debt and sells himself, his wife, his son, or his daughter for money or turns them over to forced labor, they will work for three years in the house of the man who purchased them...In the fourth year, they will be set free. (Code of Hammurabi, 117)[2]

The time limit on debt slavery was in fact a ceiling on the amount of money a debtor could be required to repay, an ancient precursor of modern bankruptcy laws. Labor was given a set loan value per annum. The term of debt servitude was determined by prorating the annual labor value to the amount owed. Three years of work equaled the debt repayment allowed by law. Whatever the amount of the original loan and its accrued interest, the debt slave had met his maximum obligation by serving the maximum term. The slate was wiped clean, and the debtor was debt free.

Exodus 21:2 and the biblical passages that build on it take Hammurabi's principle and double the length of servitude—or, to put it differently, they cut the loan value of labor in half. The "Hebrew slave" must work six years rather than three to equal the maximum payment. As we will see below, Deuteronomy 15 expands the creditor's responsibility toward the debt slave who meets his six-year obligation. Still, debt slavery in Israel was less favorable to the slave than the older Babylonian practice was.

Verses 3–4 determine the household status of wives and children of debt slaves who have worked off their debts. Whoever controlled the sexuality of the woman at the time the male debtor entered the creditor's household as a "Hebrew slave" maintains control once the debt is cleared. Verses 5–6 outline procedures for permanent enslavement if a debtor wishes to stay with his creditor after he serves the maximum term. Verse 5 gives a deeply personal rationale, but there may have been compelling economic reasons as well. As Deuteronomy 15:16 says, the debt slave may want to stay because "he is well off with you." To be a slave for life in a viable household often was better than being free to starve.

Verses 7–11 make clear that female debt slaves were treated differently than males—not surprising, given gender differentiation within the household economy. The labor value of women included their marriage value, their ability to reproduce children. Exodus 21 assumes that female debt slaves have forfeited the collateral of their

---

[2]Adapted from *ANET*, 163–64, 166–77, and Avalon.

marriage value and therefore must remain attached to the creditor's household for life: "When a man sells his daughter as a slave, she will not go out as the male slaves do" (v. 7). "Go out" refers to release at the end of the six-year limit.

In the honor/shame culture of ancient Israel, a woman who became unattached to the household of her male sexual partner was economically vulnerable. Her marriage value was seriously undermined (Exod. 22:16–17; Deut. 22:28–29). Oddly to modern eyes then, prohibiting the release of female debt slaves was a humanitarian gesture that guarded the economic security of the debt slave and protected her honor. Verses 8–11 say that she must be treated as a wife. Any failure to give her full marital rights will result in her immediate release and complete cancellation of the debt that led to her servitude (v. 11). Under no circumstances may she be sold to foreigners (v. 8b).

"Hebrew Slave" (*'ebed 'ibrî*)

"Hebrew slave" (*'ebed 'ibrî*) appears twice in the Bible, here and in Genesis 39:17, in which the wife of the Egyptian official Potiphar accuses Joseph of attempted assault. A slightly different formulation is used in the two passages that expand the slave release law in Exodus 21. Deuteronomy 15:12 speaks of the "Hebrew man or Hebrew woman who sells himself to you and serves you six years." Jeremiah 34:9 describes the release of the "male slave and female slave, the Hebrew man and Hebrew woman." The last two terms stand in apposition to the first two—"Hebrew man" equals "male slave," and "Hebrew woman" equals "female slave." And later in the same passage (Jer. 34:14), the narrator speaks of the "brother, the Hebrew, who sells himself to you and serves you six years."

The word "Hebrew" appears with a surprising lack of frequency in the Hebrew Scriptures—35 times, one of which is a personal name, "Ibri" (1 Chron. 24:27) and one of which may actually be a corrupted spelling of a verb, "to cross over" (1 Sam. 13:7).[3] In some cases, the term clearly is an ethnic designation, another word for "Israelite" or "Jew." Thus, Jonah says to the Gentile sailors on the boat to Tarshish, "I am a Hebrew, and I fear Yahweh, God of heaven, who made the sea and the dry land" (Jonah 1:9). With the exception of the slave-release passages, Jonah's statement, and an odd reference to

---

[3] For a helpful discussion of this verse, see Gottwald, *Tribes of Yahweh*, 423–24.

Abram in Genesis 14, "Hebrew" is used only in exchanges with Egyptians and Philistines. Outside of Exodus and a handful of passages in Genesis, mostly in the Joseph story, the term appears only in 1 Samuel and the two slave release passages (Deut. 15:12 and Jer. 34:9, 14) that build on Exodus 21:2.

In 1 Samuel, "Hebrew" always appears in the context of Israel's battle to free themselves from the Philistines. An Israelite uses the term on one occasion: "Saul blew the trumpet and said, 'Let the Hebrews hear!' And all Israel heard" (1 Sam. 13:3). Here "Hebrew" may be synonymous with "Israelite," but it just as easily could refer to a group of people on the battlefield other than "all Israel." Saul may be sounding the signal for the benefit of "the Hebrews," and "all Israel" heard as well. The narrator uses the term "Hebrew" twice in Samuel—if indeed the reference in 13:7 is the noun "Hebrews" and not a form of the verb "to cross over." While the soldiers of Israel hid in caves along the west bank of the Jordan River to escape destruction by the Philistine army, "Hebrews" crossed the Jordan to Gad and Gilead (13:7). Later, "the Hebrews who had formerly belonged to the Philistines and had gone up with them into battle camp now turned and joined Israel" (14:21). In these cases, it is not at all clear that "Hebrew" is synonymous with "Israelite." The "Hebrews" appear in these verses as free-floating mercenaries who ally with the Philistines and then switch loyalties to Israel when the battle shifts.

In every other case in Samuel, "Hebrew" is derogatory, an insult hurled at Israel by the Philistines (4:6; 4:9; 13:19; 14:11; 29:3). 1 Samuel 4:9 is especially revealing. The Philistine commanders, shaken by the arrival of Yahweh's ark in the battle camp of Israel, try to calm their frightened troops: "Take courage and be men, Philistines, lest you serve (ta'abdû) the Hebrews like they have served you." (Ta'abdû is from the same root as 'ebed, "slave"). Whether the term on the lips of the Philistines designates an ethnic group or a social class, it is clear that "Hebrews" are social inferiors, whose lot in life is to labor as slaves to the Philistines.

In the Joseph narrative (Gen. 37:1—50:26), "Hebrew" describes Joseph as slave (39:14, 17) and prisoner (41:15). In 40:15, Joseph says that he became a slave because he was "stolen out of the land of the Hebrews." And in 43:32, the Egyptians refuse to share a table with Joseph's brothers because Egyptians "are not allowed to eat with Hebrews—it is an abomination to them." In all these cases, "Hebrew" may be an ethnic term, but it also appears to designate an inferior social class, one suited for slavery and thus unworthy to share a table with the Egyptian lords.

Genesis 14:13 speaks of "Abram the Hebrew." This chapter is unusual for a number of reasons. Its literary features do not fit any of the primary sources scholars posit for the book of Genesis. Its narrative climaxes in the bizarre and strangely edited story of Melchizedek's blessing and Abram's "tithe" to (Jeru)salem (vv. 17–24). Its portrait of Abram as a warrior chieftain is atypical in Genesis. It is consistent, however, with what we know about the ancient Near Eastern *'apiru* or *habiru*, a term that seems to mean transient, bandit, or outlaw people—"riffraff."[4] The *'apiru* moved between the settled populations, outside the political authority of the small kingdoms and city-states that dotted the lowlands of Canaan.[5] Their social standing was precarious. They were both threatened and threatening because they lived beyond the social world of settled villages, towns, and farms.

Abram the Hebrew in Genesis 14 occupies just such a vulnerable social space. He is a nomadic resident alien who has formed protective alliances with local householders (v. 13b). His near kin, Lot and his household, resident aliens in the region of Sodom and Gomorrah, are captured and taken as a trophy of war by a raiding army. Abram musters his surprisingly large household army (318 trained soldiers, v. 14) and rescues his kin. In this story, "Hebrew" describes a "household"—really a large band of households—that occupies social space between the permanent, settled populations. The people of this household must rely on their own brute strength and on strategic alliances with local households for protection. While not portrayed as slaves, they clearly are outsiders among the native population. They may live in some sort of tenuous feudal subordination to local city-kingdoms,

---

[4] Our best sources of information about the *'apiru* are the fourteenth century B.C.E. Amarna Letters, to Egyptian Pharaoh Amenophis III (1398–1361 B.C.E.) and Pharaoh Akhenaton (1369–1353 B.C.E.) from governors they appointed in Palestine. These letters are written in an Akkadian dialect, using cuneiform rather than Egyptian hieroglyphics. Some of the governors request military assistance to protect Egyptian interests against a group of outlaws called *'apiru* who raid caravans and villages (cf. "the Song of Deborah and Barak," Judges 5, especially vv. 6–11). Others declare their independence from Egypt and join forces with the *'apiru*. The standard English translation of Amarna texts pertinent to biblical studies is found in *ANET,* 483–90.

[5] Gottwald's discussion is especially helpful (*Tribes of Yahweh,* 391–409). His chapter "Philistines as Heirs of Egyptian-Canaanite Dominion" (410–25), makes a sophisticated and appropriately nuanced case for connecting *'apiru* and "Hebrew" in several of the passages in 1 Samuel.

as implied by the confusing reference to a tithe Abram gives to the king of Sodom or Salem (v. 20b). This portrait of Abram the Hebrew is consistent with the "Hebrews" described in some of the 1 Samuel passages—armed outsiders who make temporary alliances with settled populations for mutual advantage.

Finally, the largest cluster of references to "Hebrews" comes in the book of Exodus. In every case other than the slave-release law in 21:2, "Hebrew" in Exodus describes Israel as a permanent class of forced laborers in Egypt. In the early references, "Hebrew" appears to be the Egyptians' word for Israelite slaves (1:15, 16, 19; 2:6, 7, 11, 13). From chapter 3 on, Yahweh adopts the term to describe himself as he battles Pharaoh to free Israel from Egyptian slavery: "Say to [the king of Egypt], 'Yahweh, God of the Hebrews, has met us" (3:18; cf. 5:3). In every other reference, Yahweh is described as "God of the Hebrews" in connection with the demand that Pharaoh "let my people go that they might serve me (we-ya`abdunî, the same root as `ebed, "slave").

In the ancient world, granting freedom from human servitude was often described as dedicating the freed people or region to the service of a god. Weinfeld cites a number of pertinent texts.[6] Manishtushu of Akkad (twenty-second century B.C.E.) "freed thirty-eight cities from corvée and from levy, that they might serve on behalf of the temple of the god Shamash."[7] Pepi II (ca. twenty-fourth to early twenty-second century) and Seti I (ca. 1300 B.C.E.) in Egypt make similar proclamations of freedom for the sake of service to the gods.[8] Mesopotamian kings from the third millennium through the first declared liberty so debt slaves could serve the gods.[9] Thus, when Enmetena of Lagash (twenty-fifth century) "established liberation for Lagash" and "instituted liberation for the interest on barley," he "restored [the people] to the goddess Inanna of Uruk...to the god Utu of Larsa...[and] to Lugalemush of Emush."[10] People who were dedicated as slaves to a god were released from service to human lords.

---

[6]Weinfeld, *Social Justice*, 16–17, 78–83, 97–131. See especially his final chapter, "Israelites as Servants of YHWH, and the Land of Israel as the Land of YHWH: On the Nature of the Judicial Pattern" (231–47).

[7]Ibid.,16.

[8]Ibid., 16–17.

[9]Ibid., 78–83.

[10]Ibid., 78.

This is the idea behind Leviticus 25:42, which prohibits the permanent enslavement of Israelites: "They are my slaves (*'ebaday*), whom I brought out of the land of Egypt. They certainly must not be sold as slaves" (cf. 25:55).

In Exodus, "Hebrew" is inextricably bound to slavery and to freedom. In the first instance, Israelites as "Hebrews" suffer seemingly permanent slavery to the Egyptians. In the second instance, Yahweh as "God of the Hebrews" liberates them from slavery to Pharaoh by dedicating these Israelite "Hebrews" to divine servitude.

So, in the broader narrative context of Exodus, "Hebrew slave" in 21:2 is both redundant and self-contradictory. A "Hebrew" *is* a "slave," bought by Yahweh, dedicated to God's service, and therefore freed from all human bondage. "Hebrew slave" is a theologically loaded term that rhetorically circumscribes debt slavery in Israel. By alluding to Israel's exodus and election to divine service, the text suggests that a debt slave in Israel cannot be enslaved forever. The abolitionist logic of Leviticus 25:42 quoted above is implicit in the very term "Hebrew slave." Dedicated to Yahweh, God of the Hebrews, the "Hebrew slave" cannot be enslaved by any earthly power. The character of Yahweh and the nature of God's relationship with Israel are at stake in the treatment of the "Hebrew slave."

Deuteronomy 15:1–18

Deuteronomy 15 expands the Hebrew slave law of Exodus 21:2 and attaches a new, but related law, seventh-year debt release (*shemittah*).

Though possibly originating in the time of the Judean monarchy, the seventh-year laws of Deuteronomy 15:1–18 are now set in a book edited from the perspective of Babylonian exile, anticipating the return of deportees to Jerusalem and the restoration of Judah. The readers of this final version of Deuteronomy are invited to enter the narrative world of the book's main characters, the preacher Moses and his audience Israel, camped on the east bank of the Jordan River, just outside the promised land, waiting to go in.

Like all the Bible's historical books, Deuteronomy telescopes history. Narrative time is not the real time of the author or the ancient readers, but it speaks to their time. Any given passage of Deuteronomy thus operates in multiple historical dimensions all at once. It occupies the narrative time of Israel's legendary nomadic past, before the people first entered the land. But the social structure reflected in the laws that make up Deuteronomy's core is that of settled farmers, not wandering nomads. Deuteronomy speaks to an agrarian society headed by a monarch (17:14–20) and organized religiously around a royal temple (e.g., 12:2–14). In Deuteronomy, Israel stands *outside* the land as a ragtag army of homeless people waiting to get in, and simultaneously *inside* the land as an established nation with a fully developed, agriculturally based royal system. Furthermore, they stand outside the land in two vastly different eras, before Israel's native monarchy began (4:1) and after it was destroyed more than four centuries later (4:25–31; 28:36–37, 64–67; 29:1—39:20). Israel is waiting to enter the promised land for the first time and for the second. The ancient readers of Deuteronomy stand at the end of a wilderness journey from Egyptian slavery and also from Babylonian exile.

In Deuteronomy, narrative Israel embodies centuries of experience before, during, and after the Davidic monarchy. Pinpointing the original date of the seventh-year legislation in Deuteronomy 15 is, therefore, virtually impossible. We can say, however, that these laws make sense only for an agrarian society with a fairly well-developed system of interest lending. Whether they originated before or after 586 B.C.E., they reflect the social and economic conditions of monarchy.

They Will Not Go Out Empty-Handed

> If your kin, the Hebrew man or Hebrew woman, sell themselves to you and serve you six years, in the seventh year you must let them go free from you. And when you let them go free from you, you must not let them go out empty-handed. Adorn them with provisions from your flock, your threshing-floor, and your wine-vat. Give them what Yahweh your God has blessed you with. And remember that you were a slave (*'ebed*) in the land of Egypt, and Yahweh your God bought your freedom. Therefore, I am commanding you to do this thing today. But if [the slave] says to you, "I will not leave you" because he loves you and your household, since being with you is good for him, you must take the awl and put it through his ear and the doorpost. Then he will be a permanent slave (*'ebed 'ôlam*) to you. Do the same for your female slave. Do not consider it a hardship when you send them out free from you, because they have served you six years for double the worth of a hired laborer, while Yahweh

your God has blessed you in everything you have done."(Deut. 15:12–18)

This passage builds on Exodus 21:2–11, but expands seventh-year emancipation to cover female debt slaves as well (vv. 12, 17b). The release of female slaves changes the rationale for voluntary permanent slavery in Exodus 21:5–6. In Exodus, the permanent slave is motivated by love of wife and children who must stay in the creditor's household. In Deuteronomy, slave wives "go out" with their husbands. So debt slaves who choose to become permanent slaves do so, not to keep their families intact, but because they have greater economic security as slaves than as free persons (v. 16).

Deuteronomy's revision of the law in Exodus 21 expands the creditor's responsibility toward the debtor once the debt is paid. At the end of the six-year term, debt slaves must not go out "empty-handed." The creditor must "adorn them" with provisions of grain, wine, and cattle. The verb I have translated "adorn" literally means, "to hang a necklace," painting a vivid image of the newly freed slave luxuriously draped in wealth, dangling like precious ornaments around the neck.

The rationale for this lavish send-off is economic and theological. The debtor who has served the six-year maximum has in fact given service worth "double the wage of a wage laborer" (v. 18). Perhaps the deuteronomic author is aware of the more generous policy of Hammurabi's law. In any case, the deuteronomists believe that the creditor who receives the maximum term of service has been more than sufficiently compensated for the original loan. Sharing the surplus is only fair.

A subtle change in the wording of the basic law in verse 12 hints at the theological rationale stated explicitly in verse 15: "Remember that you were a slave in the land of Egypt, and Yahweh your God bought your freedom." The older Hebrew slave law in Exodus 21:2 says that after six years of debt servitude the male slave "will go out" (*yetse'*) free. Deuteronomy changes the verb—a small shift in wording, a giant leap in rhetoric. In the seventh year, "you must let them go" (*teshallehenû*) free.

The verb translated "to let go" (*shalah*) is the word used throughout the exodus narratives to describe Yahweh's demand that Pharaoh liberate Israelite slaves: "Let my people go!"[11] But it also means "to stretch out" or "extend," as in, "to stretch out the hand." Yahweh and Moses "stretch out" the hand to perform miracles and to bring plagues on Egypt.[12] Finally, Moses is "sent" (*shalah*) by Yahweh to liberate Israel from Egyptian slavery (Exod. 3:10–15; 4:13, 28; 5:22; 7:16).

The wording of the Hebrew slave law reminds Israel that all Israelites are "slaves" bought by Yahweh, bonded to God's service, and therefore freed from human bondage. The use of the word "let go," in the basic law associates the creditor with all three main characters in the exodus saga: Pharaoh, Moses, and Yahweh. Pharaoh had the political power but not the political will to "let Yahweh's people go" (*shalah*). Yahweh "sent" (*shalah*) Moses to bring Israel out of bondage. When Pharaoh's heart was hardened and he refused to honor God's request, Yahweh, acting through Moses, "stretched out his hand" (*shalah*) and brought devastating plagues against Egypt. The choice of *shalah* thus contains an implicit threat. Only a fool would repeat Pharaoh's hard-hearted mistake. Not surprisingly then, Deuteronomy warns the well-to-do Israelite not to be hard-hearted[13] toward those in need (15:7). The fate of Pharaoh at the hand of Yahweh, God of the Hebrews, may well await the hard-hearted creditor who will not let the Hebrew slave go when his or her term of service is fulfilled.

Finally, the deuteronomic author connects the Hebrew slave law with the exodus narrative by providing that the slave not go out "empty-handed" (*rêqam*). Exodus 3:21–22 says that the Israelites will plunder Egypt when they are finally freed from slavery. "When you leave, you will not leave empty-handed (*rêqam*). Each woman will ask her neighbor…for silver and gold jewelry and clothing, and you will put them on your sons and daughters, and you will plunder the Egyptians." The prediction is fulfilled in 12:35–36 in the narrative context of Passover and the feast of unleavened bread. *Rêqam* appears

---

[11] Exodus 3:20; 4:21, 23; 5:1–2; 6:1, 10; 7:2, 14, 16, 26–27 [Heb]=8:1–2 [Eng]; 8:4, 16–17, 24–25 [Heb]=8:8, 20–21, 28–29 [Eng]; 9:1–2, 13, 17, 28, 35; 10:3–4, 7, 10, 20, 27; 11:1, 10; 12:33; 13:15, 17; 14:5.

[12] Exodus 3:20; 4:4; 9:14–15; 15:7; cf. 23:27–28; 33:2. The postexilic Priestly writer (P) prefers the verb *natah* for this idiom (Exod. 7:19; 8:1–2, 12–13 [Heb]=8:5–6, 16–17 [Eng]). The preexilic Yahwist (J) uses both (*natah*: 9:22–23; 10:22; 14:16, 21, 26–27; *shalah*: see above).

[13] The verb is different here (*'amats*) than it is in Exodus (normally *hazaq* or *kabed*, though once *qashah*, 7:3), but the meaning is the same. *Hazaq*: Exod. 4:21; 7:13, 22; 8:15 [Heb]=8:19 [Eng]; 9:12, 35; 10:20, 27; 11:10; 14:4, 8, 17. *Kabed*: 7:14; 8:11, 28 [Heb]=8:15, 32 [Eng]; 9:7, 34; 10:1.

two other times in Exodus (23:15 and 34:20) and once in Deuteronomy (16:16) in connection with the feast of unleavened bread: "No one should appear before [Yahweh] empty-handed." So all these passages are rooted in the liberation story, particularly the night of the final plague when Israel was finally released.

The plundering of Egypt may be disconcerting to modern readers, but the ancient ethics of it are clarified in the one other pentateuchal story where *rêqam* appears. In Genesis 31:42, Jacob speaks to his father-in-law, Laban, whom he has served, in effect, as a debt slave to work off the bride-price for Rachel and Leah and to purchase flocks. When Jacob's extraordinarily long term of service is fulfilled (20 years, vv. 38, 41), Laban is reluctant to release him. Jacob finally flees Laban's household under cover of darkness. When Laban catches him, Jacob accuses his father-in-law: "If the God of my father, the God of Abraham and the fear of Isaac, had not been with me, even now you would have sent me out (*shalah*) empty-handed (*rêqam*). But God saw my affliction and the toil of my hand and issued a rebuke last night." Jacob's assessment that Laban had tried to cheat him (cf. 31:7) is correct. Laban and his adult sons resented sharing household wealth with Jacob (31:1–2), even though Jacob made them prosper. Jacob rightly claimed a share of Laban the creditor's household wealth. He should not "go out empty-handed" at the end of his term.

Likewise, Egyptian "plunder" in Exodus 3:21–22 and 12:35–36 is the rightful due of debt slaves who have made their stingy creditors prosper. Egypt grudgingly "let Israel go," and Israel took by subterfuge what they should have been given gladly. As Deuteronomy says, "when you let them go free, you must not let them go out empty-handed. Adorn them with provisions from your flock, your threshing-floor, and your wine-vat. Give them what Yahweh your God has blessed you with" (15:13–14).

In Deuteronomy, as in Exodus, the treatment of the Hebrew slave is tied to Israel's sacred narrative of liberation from Egypt. Fundamental issues of God's sovereignty in the world and Israel's identity as Yahweh's liberated people are at stake. As Yahweh showed mercy and generosity toward enslaved Israel, the Israelite creditor must show mercy and generosity toward the Hebrew slave.

Summary

The Bible borrows from ancient Near Eastern legal tradition to set humane limits on the forced servitude of debtors in default. Following ancient practice, Exodus 21 and Deuteronomy 15 set a cap on the total amount a debt slave must repay and calculate a maximum term of servitude by prorating the value of a year's labor. The Babylonian Code of Hammurabi is more generous to the debt slave than the biblical texts are, setting the cap at three years.

Deuteronomy and Exodus differ in their treatment of female slaves, though both are primarily concerned with the long-term welfare of enslaved women. Exodus requires the creditor to treat the female debt slave like a wife or daughter-in-law. Deuteronomy emancipates female slaves along with male slaves at the end of six years. But Deuteronomy expands the Exodus slave law, requiring the creditor to set the debt slave free with a lavish severance package.

In various ways, Exodus and Deuteronomy connect the emancipation of debt slaves with the sacred narrative of Israel's liberation from Egypt. The clearest connection is the description of the debt slave as a "Hebrew slave." By observing the terms of the Hebrew slave law, Israel celebrates the character of Yahweh, divine redeemer and savior of slaves.

4

RELEASE THE DEBT!
RELEASE THE WEALTH!

L ike the Hebrew slave laws, the release laws examined in this chapter are rooted in the culture of mutual support, characteristic of the household-based economies of the ancient Near East. Deuteronomy's debt release is based on royal proclamations of liberty, common in the ancient world. It introduces a striking innovation, however, that makes it unique in antiquity. The accounts of release by the Judean king Zedekiah and the Persian governor Nehemiah are similar to royal proclamations elsewhere. Finally, Exodus 23 advocates a seventh-year release of agrarian produce for the support of the poor.

A Release for Yahweh

Every seven years you must grant a release. This is the manner of the release: everyone who holds a debt claim against a neighbor must release it. He must not press his neighbor, his kin, because a release for Yahweh has been declared. You may press the foreigner, but whatever you have against your kin, you must release from your control. (Deut. 15:1–3)

37

Deuteronomy's law of release is rooted in common royal practice in the ancient world. From the third millennium on, Mesopotamian kings made proclamations of release, usually at the beginning of their rule. These decrees of *misharum* (cf. the Hebrew *mîsharîm,* "uprightness") or *andurarum* (cf. the Hebrew *derôr,* "liberty")[1] were ancient equivalents of tax cuts and pork-barrel spending, intended to curry favor and boost the political power of the new king. Declarations varied in scope and content but included canceling debts, returning ancestral property lost through foreclosure, freeing debt and permanent slaves, forgiving taxes and state labor, releasing prisoners, returning exiles to native lands, and making contributions to temples.

Moshe Weinfeld collects several examples. Enmetena of Lagash (ca. 2430 B.C.E.) restored household property and instituted debt relief.[2] About three centuries later, Manishtushu released 38 cities from state labor and military draft obligations.[3] Ishme-Dagan of Isin (1953–1935 B.C.E.) released the temple city Nippur from taxes and military draft.[4] His successor, Lipit-Ishtar (1934–1924 B.C.E.) reduced the amount of state labor required of households in Nippur, Ur, Isin, Sumer, and Akkad.[5] Kurigalzu released Babylon from state labor in the fourteenth century.[6] Debts were canceled by local princes in the Assyrian colonies of Cappadocia (twentieth and nineteenth centuries) and in Assyria itself by Ilushuma and Erishum I.[7] One of the Mari letters from a royal official to Zimri-lim (ca. 1775–1768 B.C.E.) speaks of a slave release as part of the *andurarum* the king had proclaimed.[8] The Hittite king Hatushili I (mid-sixteenth century) freed slaves.[9] In Sumer, Urukagina's reform (2370 B.C.E.) freed prisoners held for debt, back taxes, theft, and murder.[10]

---

[1]Weinfeld, *Social Justice,* 75–96. *Misharum* means "to walk straight." *Andurarum* basically means "to roll," as in to roll freely unencumbered.

[2]Ibid., 78–79.

[3]Ibid., 80.

[4]Ibid., 82.

[5]Ibid., 83.

[6]Ibid., 80.

[7]Ibid., 92. Debt cancellation is described as "erasing the tablets" or "washing away the copper," apparently referring to the tablets on which the debts were written.

[8]Ibid., 88.

[9]Ibid., 92.

[10]Ibid., 81.

Several sale documents from Mari[11] and Hana[12] contain legal provisions to bypass royal declarations of release: "This field will not be subject to *andurarum*."[13] Sale documents from Nuzi specify that transactions were completed "after the proclamation"[14] to prevent anyone from claiming that the terms of the deal were voided by royal decree. Slave documents from Kalah and Nineveh in the Neo-Assyrian period make provision for a royal *andurarum* decree: "If these [slaves] shall be released in the liberation [*duraru*], Bel-ali [the seller] shall return the silver to its owner."[15]

Similar royal decrees are recorded in Egypt[16] and in the reform of Solon (594–593 B.C.E.) in Greece. He released slaves and canceled debt and liens on property.[17] Royal releases are recorded in Persia, Greece, and the Hellenistic kingdoms through the Roman period.[18] The Rosetta Stone is a celebration of the release that King Ptolemy V Epiphanes declared in 197 B.C.E. at his coronation.[19] He forgave back taxes, canceled debts to the crown, freed prisoners, pardoned rebels, and made grants to temples.[20] The proclamation of Ptolemy VIII Euergetes II (118 B.C.E.) at the end of a civil war released prisoners (except murderers and blasphemers), canceled debt to the king, stopped tax collection, and abolished forced state labor.[21]

Loans to "Foreigners" and Near Kin

The seventeenth-century proclamation of the Babylonian king Ammisaduqa[22] provides an interesting parallel with the distinction

---

[11]Ibid., 86–87. Documents from the period of Yahdun-lim (1809–1797 B.C.E.), Shamshi-Addu (1827–1810 B.C.E.), and Zimri-lim (1775–1768 B.C.E.) contain provisions to circumvent declarations of *andurarum*.

[12]Ibid., 91, n. 72.

[13]Ibid., 86.

[14]*ANET*, 219–220. See also Weinfeld, *Social Justice*, 93–94,158.

[15]J. N. Postgate, *The Governor's Palace Archive* (London: British School of Archaeology in Iraq, 1973), no. 248, p. 22; Weinfeld, *Social Justice*, 94.

[16]Weinfeld, *Social Justice*, 140–41: a hymn celebrating the coronation of Ramses IV speaks of fugitives returning home and prisoners released. A hymn to Merneptah says, "He liberated prisoners in every district, gave gifts to temples... had the property of the great restored, and the poor returned to their villages" (ibid., 143–44).

[17]Ibid., 145, 170.

[18]Ibid., 145–51.

[19]R. S. Bagnall and P. Derow, *Greek Historical Documents: The Hellenistic Period* (Chico, Calif.: Scholars Press, 1981), no. 137, pp. 226–30.

[20]Weinfeld, *Social Justice*, 147.

[21]Ibid., 147–48, 173–74.

[22]Ibid., 89–90, 163–69; *ANET*, 526–28.

between local and "foreign" debtors in the release law in Deuteronomy 15:2–3. Ammisaduqa's decree erases overdue taxes, cancels state and private debts, frees debt slaves, gives targeted tax cuts, and exempts citizens from military draft. Paragraph 3 of this twenty-two-paragraph decree "breaks the tablet" (i.e., expunges the record) on interest loans of "grain or silver" given *to* an Akkadian or Amorite (i.e., a native). Paragraph 8 exempts loans given *by* an Akkadian or Amorite for trade. The latter tablets "shall not be broken."

Deuteronomy 15:2–3 also makes a distinction between loans, canceling debts of "your neighbor, your kin," but exempting loans given to "foreigners." The distinction is not merely ethnic. "Your neighbor, your kin," is clan language, evoking the culture of mutual support within and between households. Loans to "your neighbor, your kin" are subsistence loans to households that fall within the creditor's zone of responsibility, that is, a household in the creditor's own village or clan. The word in verse 3 is *nokrî*, "foreigner," not *ger*, "resident alien." Allied with local households and perhaps even attached to them in some sort of service arrangement, the resident alien is part of the network of mutual support between village households. So subsistence loans to resident aliens are more likely included among the loans to "your neighbor, your kin" in verse 2 than among the loans to "foreigners" in verse 3. The issue is not the ethnicity of the borrower, but the nature of the loan. Subsistence help for (foreign) travelers was offered as a gift, not a loan—an act of hospitality, not a debt to be repaid. Loans to "foreigners"—that is, nonresidents who fall outside the network of clan support—are by their very nature trade loans. Deuteronomy, like Ammisaduqa's decree, is distinguishing between subsistence loans and commercial loans.

Verse 9 makes clear that loans to "your neighbor, your kin," subject to seventh-year release, are subsistence loans. "Be careful that you don't entertain a worthless thought, thinking that the seventh year, the year of release, is drawing near. So your needy kin becomes hideous to you and you do not give to him, prompting him to call out to Yahweh so it will be counted against you as sin." Instead, the well-off are told not to be "hard-hearted" or "tightfisted" toward the needy neighbor (v. 7). Rather, "you must open your hand" to them, lending whatever they require to meet the need (v. 8).

Closing the hand in verse 7 and opening it in verse 8 refer back to the basic release law in verse 2 and to the root meaning of the Hebrew word "release," *shemittah*: "Everyone who holds a debt claim against a neighbor must release it" (v. 2). The verb "release!" (*shamôt*) is from the same root as the noun "release" (*shemittah*). Its basic meaning is "to loosen" or "to drop." The idea is that the one who holds the loan must "loosen his grip" (literally, "release his hand") on the debtor's obligation to repay. He must "drop it." The law of release, *shemittah*, then is the exact opposite of being tightfisted toward needy neighbors. It is a concrete gesture of opening the hand to the poor.

In Mesopotamia, unpredictable royal proclamations of liberty added an element of uncertainty to financial transactions, particularly those related to debts and slavery. As we saw above, several documents have survived that include provisions to soften the commercial disruption caused by royal *andurarum* decrees. Only Deuteronomy 15, however, seeks to establish a regular cycle of debt release.

The literary connection in Deuteronomy 15 between debt release and the Hebrew slave law suggests that the seven-year cycle may have been set as an analogy to the cap on debt servitude. Whatever its origin, however, the regularity of the deuteronomic practice reduced uncertainty. Everyone knew exactly when release would be proclaimed. But certitude created its own problem: Creditors were hesitant to grant loans the year before seventh-year release. Verse 9 attempts to correct the problem by moral sanction: Needy kin may "call out to Yahweh," and "it will be counted against you as sin."

Moral sanction was insufficient to keep credit flowing, however, as Judean society in the second temple period became more urbanized and the economy more commercial. Subsistence loans for the poor dried up in the sixth year. To remedy the situation, Rabbi Hillel instituted a legal bypass, the *prosbul*,[23] which turned the debt over to the courts before the year of release, with the reasoning that *shemittah* is binding on individual Jews, but not on the courts. The courts could collect the loan on the creditor's behalf. *Prosbul* proves that seventh-year debt release was practiced, albeit reluctantly.

A Disastrous Double Cross

> The word that came to Jeremiah from Yahweh after King Zedekiah made a covenant with all the people in Jerusalem, proclaiming liberty *[derôr]* for them, that each one would set his male and female slave free—the Hebrew man and the Hebrew woman—that none of them would enslave a Jew,

---

[23]See Mishnah, Sheviit 10:3, and Talmud Gittin 36a.

their kin. All the princes and all the people obeyed—everyone who entered the covenant to set their male and female slaves free—so that none of them would be enslaved again. They obeyed and released.

And then they turned around and forced the male and female slaves they had set free to return. They bound them by force as male and female slaves.

The word of Yahweh came to Jeremiah from Yahweh: Thus says Yahweh God of Israel:"I made a covenant with your ancestors the day I brought them out of the land of Egypt from the house of slaves: "Every seven years each of you must release his kin, the Hebrew who sold himself to you and has served you six years. You must set him free from you!"

But your ancestors did not obey me; they did not listen.

You, however, turned and did the right thing in my view, proclaiming liberty [derôr], each for his neighbor. You made a covenant in my presence in the house that is called by my name.

But you turned and profaned my name! Each of you forced his male and female slaves whom you had set free for life to return! And you bound them by force to be male and female slaves for you!

Therefore, thus says Yahweh: You did not obey me and proclaim liberty [derôr], each for his kin and neighbor. So now I am proclaiming liberty [derôr] for you, declares Yahweh—[liberty] to the sword, to pestilence, and famine! I will make you a horror to all the kingdoms of the earth! (Jer. 34:8–22)

Zedekiah's proclamation of liberty is recorded only in Jeremiah 34.[24] Besides its unique content, the narrative has several curious

---

[24]Good scholarly treatments of this passage are found in M. David, "The Manumission of Slaves Under Zedekiah (A Contribution to the Laws about Hebrew Slaves)," *Oudtestamentische Studiën* 5 (1948); N. P. Lemche, "The Manumission of Slaves—The Fallow Year—The Sabbatical Year—The Jobel Year," *Vetus Testamentum* 26 (1976): 38–59; and N. Sarna, "Zedekiah's Emancipation of Slaves and the Sabbatical Year," *Orient and Occident: Essays presented to Cyrus H. Gordon on the occasion of his sixty-fifth birthday* Alter Orient und Altes Testament 22; ed. H. A. Hoffner (Neukirchen: Neukirchener Verlag, 1973), 143–49. For a completely different take, see Robert Carroll, *Jeremiah*, Old Testament Library (Philadelphia: Westminster, 1986), 643–50. Carroll sees the story as a nonhistorical postexilic literary construction dependent on the jubilee tradition in Leviticus 25, which envisions the abolition of debt slavery, and the release in Deuteronomy 15, which limits the impact of debt slavery.

features. To begin with, it immediately follows a surprising oracle (34:2–5) that predicts Zedekiah's exile to Babylon (vv. 2–3) and his eventual return to Jerusalem, unharmed: "You will not die by the sword, but will die in peace" and receive a proper royal funeral in Jerusalem (vv. 4–5). This appears to contradict his fate in verses 8–22 and in Jeremiah 39:4–7 and 2 Kings 25:4–7, which describe Zedekiah's brutal torture at Riblah after he was captured fleeing besieged Jerusalem. According to these versions of the story, Zedekiah was forced to witness the murder of all his children before he was blinded and taken away in fetters to Babylon, where he disappeared from history.

Jeremiah 34:8–22 is influenced by the deuteronomistic literary tradition[25] but offers a unique interpretation of the destruction of Jerusalem in 586 B.C.E. that contradicts the closing chapters of 2 Kings, the deuteronomists' definitive statement on royal Judah's fall. There, Jerusalem fell because Manasseh (21:10–15; 23:26–27; 24:3), all the kings of Judah (23:32, 37), or all the people of Judah (17:19–20; 22:16–17; 24:20) refused to follow deuteronomic orthodoxy, which advocated the worship of Yahweh alone and the centralization of all cult practices in Jerusalem. Jeremiah 34, by contrast, says that Jerusalem fell because Zedekiah and the people violated their own liberty decree, voluntarily offered and then withdrawn.

This interpretation is inconsistent, not only with Kings, but also with the bulk of Jeremiah. Elsewhere in Jeremiah, Judah is condemned for corruption, injustice, idolatry, and rebellion against Yahweh. One other passage in Jeremiah offers an unconventional explanation for the destruction of Jerusalem. Jeremiah 17:27 points to improper sabbath observance as the reason for Jerusalem's demise: "If you don't obey me, keeping the sabbath day holy, not lifting and carrying a burden through the gates of Jerusalem on the sabbath day, then I will kindle a fire against its gates that will consume the palaces of Jerusalem and not be quenched." Jeremiah 17:27 resonates with the explanation in Leviticus 26:34–35, where Babylonian exile is an opportunity for the land to "enjoy its sabbaths" and get "the rest it did not have on

---

[25]Most twentieth-century Jeremiah scholarship builds on the sources mapped out by Bernard Duhm and Sigmund Mowinckel, which include a major deuteronomic strand in Jeremiah. Several important essays are reprinted in Leo G. Perdue and Brian W. Kovacs, eds., *A Prophet to the Nations: Essays in Jeremiah Studies* (Winona Lake, Ind.: Eisenbrauns, 1984). Walter Brueggemann's *A Commentary on Jeremiah: Exile and Homecoming* (Grand Rapids: Eerdmans, 1998) is worthwhile. Unlike R. E. Clements when he wrote his popular commentary *Jeremiah*, Interpretation; (Atlanta: John Knox, 1988), Brueggemann had the benefit of having read Robert Carroll's excellent commentary.

your sabbaths when you were living on it." All these passages are late—exilic at the earliest. Zedekiah's decree and the sabbath oracle in Jeremiah 17 probably reflect theological concerns of the second temple period.[26]

There are a number of reasons to doubt the historicity of Zedekiah's proclamation. For one thing, it is difficult to explain the motivation for the slave release or its rescission. Most scholars date Zedekiah's proclamation by the phrase at the end of 34:21, which describes the Babylonian army "that has retreated from you" and will return at Yahweh's command (v. 22). This phrase is paired with 37:5–11, which speaks of a Babylonian retreat from Jerusalem in the face of Egyptian troop movements toward Judah. So the narrative setting of the judgment oracles in 34:12–22 is thought to be a temporary lull in the Babylonian siege of Jerusalem, induced by the appearance of Egyptian soldiers sometime after Zedekiah's rebellion began and before it ended in 586 B.C.E.

This historical setting begs the question of motive. Was the original decree a cynical populist ploy on the part of Zedekiah and the wealthy creditors of Jerusalem at a moment of crisis? If so, to what end? Emancipation did not increase the pool of Judean soldiers, because every male in the household was responsible for defense—slave or free. Emancipated slaves might well be more highly motivated soldiers, but Jerusalem was under siege, not marching into battle out in the field. How exactly does the status of Hebrew slaves affect conditions inside the wall one way or the other?

Some interpreters think the king was motivated by religious considerations. By finally observing slave release, Zedekiah hoped to curry favor with Yahweh, who in turn would lift the siege. But Zedekiah's proclamation is not consistent with the Hebrew slave law in Exodus 21 or the slave law and debt release in Deuteronomy 15. Even if Zedekiah was attempting to appease Yahweh by instituting a deuteronomic social reform, why tempt fate by reneging as soon as Yahweh lifts the siege? In the final analysis, it is difficult to see how this emancipation helps Jerusalem's elite under Babylonian siege, or why they would suddenly reverse themselves and rescind it.

We are better off dropping the question of historical setting and motivation and following the lead of the text itself, which offers no explanation for Zedekiah's decree or the wealthy creditors' double

---

[26]Carroll's interpretation is right on target here (*Jeremiah*, 646–50).

cross. Verse 8 simply reports that King Zedekiah made a covenant with all the people in Jerusalem to proclaim liberty. Verse 10 reports that all the slaveholders "obeyed and released." And, without explanation, verse 11 says that later "they turned around and forced the male and female slaves they had set free to return."

Though clearly related to debt release and the Hebrew slave law in Deuteronomy 15, Zedekiah's decree and Yahweh's response to the double cross merge the two deuteronomic laws and introduce jubilee tradition from Leviticus 25. Verse 9 speaks of setting free their "male and female" Hebrew slaves, drawing from Deuteronomy's version of the Hebrew slave law. But Hebrew slaves in Deuteronomy and Exodus are released individually, not all at once. The language of Jeremiah 34:14, "every seventh year," is drawn directly from Deuteronomy 15:1, which describes debt cancellation, not slave release. Jeremiah 34 has merged the general debt release every seven years in Deuteronomy 15:1–3 with the Hebrew slave law in Deuteronomy 15:12–18.

This deuteronomic hybrid is further modified by the jubilee tradition in Leviticus, which abolishes slavery altogether: "If any [of your kin] become so impoverished that they sell themselves to you, you must not make them serve as slaves" (Lev. 25:39). "They are my slaves whom I brought out of the land of Egypt. They certainly must not be sold as slaves" (25:42; cf. v. 55). Zedekiah's proclamation, like jubilee, is a liberty (*derôr*; cf. Lev. 25:10) instituted so that "none of them would enslave a Jew, their kin" (Jer. 34:9), and "none of them would be enslaved again" (v. 10). Exodus 21 and Deuteronomy 15 limit the harsh effects of debt slavery. Jeremiah 34, like Leviticus 25, seeks total abolition.

The story of Zedekiah's ill-fated decree thus does what later generations of interpreters would do: It thoroughly mixes various sabbath-year and jubilee traditions. These verses serve, then, not as the historical account of an actual event, but as a moral lesson on the evils of debt slavery and the seriousness of a covenant sworn in the presence of Yahweh.[27] Judah's worst disaster is tied to the treachery of the wealthy who give false hope to the poor, only to dash it when doing so proves convenient or profitable.

Zedekiah's decree is the kind of thing kings did in the ancient Near East. And the creditors' heartless enslavement of those they had promised to free is all too familiar. Whether the specific event actually

<hr />

[27]See Carroll's helpful discussion, 648–49.

happened, Zedekiah's decree and the wealthy's double cross are typical. The narrative tells a true, though possibly unhistorical, story that teaches an important moral lesson. By tying the broken promise of liberty to the destruction of Jerusalem, Jeremiah 34 highlights the seriousness of justice for the economically vulnerable and faithfulness to covenants undertaken on their behalf. It is especially noteworthy that the covenant violated is a covenant between people of power to benefit people who are powerless. Yahweh takes social justice for the poor very seriously. Failure to follow through on just commitments leads to utter disaster.

Hearing the Outcry

There was a great outcry of the people and their wives against their Jewish kin. There were those who were saying, "… We must get grain to eat and live!" There were those who were saying, "We are having to mortgage our fields, our vineyards, and our houses to get grain during the famine!" There were those who were saying, "We are having to borrow money on our fields and vineyards to pay the king's taxes! Our flesh is like the flesh of our kin, our children like their children; but look, we are forcing our sons and daughters to be slaves. Some of our daughters have been raped, and we are powerless [to do anything] about it! And our fields and vineyards belong to others!"

I was very angry when I heard their outcry…I thought it over, and brought charges against the nobles and the rulers. I said to them, "You are each taking interest from your own kin!" I called a large assembly against them, and I said to them, "As much as we have been able, we have bought back our own Jewish kin who had been sold to the nations. But you have been selling your own kin, who must then be bought back by us!" They were silent and could not find a word.

Then I said, "This thing you are doing is not good! Will you not, in fear of our God, walk away from the taunts of the nations, our enemies? What's more, I, my brothers, and my servants are lending them money and grain. Let's abandon this interest-taking! Return their fields to them today, their vineyards, their olive orchards, and their houses, along with the interest[28] on money and grain, wine and oil that you have been exacting from them!" And they said, "We will return[29] (it), and we will not seek (anything else) from them. We will do just as you say."

Then I summoned the priests, and I made them swear to act according to this promise. Then I shook out the fold of my garment and said, "Thus may God shake out from home and property anyone who does not keep this promise. Thus may they be shaken out and emptied!"

And the whole assembly said, "Amen!" They praised Yahweh, and the people acted according to this promise. (Neh. 5:1–13)

The people's complaint to Nehemiah offers a textbook case of the destructive social impact of the interest debt system that flourished under ancient monarchies. Non-wealthy households find it impossible to meet their tax obligations to the monarchy—in this case, the Persian Empire—and still feed their families, especially in bad agricultural years. They are forced to borrow money and grain at interest from politically influential, rich landowners. To qualify for loans, debtors must put up household property and labor as collateral. Eventually unable to repay the principal and interest, debtors lose their collateral, forfeiting ancestral property and lapsing into debt slavery. The rich get richer, adding land and labor to their household wealth, while the poor lose everything.

Nehemiah's solution to the people's complaint is related not so much to the Hebrew slave law (Exod. 21:2; Deut. 15:12–18) or debt release (Deut. 15:1–3) as to the deuteronomic and Priestly prohibitions on interest lending (Deut. 23:20–21 [19–20]; Lev. 25:36–37). Both traditions prohibit interest loans to "kin." Deuteronomy 23:21 [20], however, explicitly allows interest lending to "the foreigner." As I argued above, the distinction between loans to "kin" and "foreigners" is not primarily ethnic. Loans to kin are subsistence loans. Loans to foreigners are trade loans for commerce.

Nehemiah's reform, carried out in a community under siege from hostile forces opposed to Jerusalem's reconstruction, gives a decidedly

---

[28]Literally, "the hundredth."

[29]*Nashib* is delightfully ambiguous: "We will repent/turn around" or "We will restore."

ethnic cast to the interest-debt laws—though it is clear that the loans under dispute are subsistence loans. Greedy profiteering by wealthy households at the expense of their needy "Jewish kin" opens the community of returning exiles to "the taunts of the nations, our enemies" (v. 9), local populations who oppose their building project.[30] It is important to note that "ethnicity" in this regard is based on shared experience rather than bloodline. "The Jews" are those Judeans who had been deported to Babylonia in 597 and 586 B.C.E. (cf. Neh. 10:28–31; Ezra 6:21; 9:1—10:44) and have now returned to Jerusalem to rebuild. They now consider themselves to be ethnically distinct from those Judeans who never went into exile, the so-called "peoples of the land" (Neh. 10:28–31).

It is interesting that Nehemiah brings formal charges against Jewish nobles and officers (5:7) but relies on the culture of honor and shame rather than legal precedent to make his case. He appeals not to pentateuchal law, but to the people's sense of honor. These wealthy creditors have brought shame upon their own community. And, to make matters worse, they have done so during a time of crisis, when the community is under external threat. Nehemiah's critique of their unscrupulous profiteering and the debt reforms he forces them to accept are rooted in the household–based culture of social solidarity. The principles are Jewish and biblical, but not peculiarly so. Nehemiah's reform is reported with a distinctively biblical flair, however, connected rhetorically with Israel's broader sacred narrative.

Nehemiah's symbolic act at the end of the oath-taking is particularly interesting: "Then I shook out the fold of my garment…" The precise meaning of the Hebrew word *hotsnî*, "fold of my garment," is uncertain, but the root word seems to describe the act of clutching and carrying in folded arms. A modern equivalent for the noun would be a purse slung over the shoulder or the inner pocket of a sports coat, a hidden place "close to the vest" and "next to the heart" where you might keep a wallet. Nehemiah is turning his pockets inside out and shaking them clean. Those who swore the oath that day would never again "make one red cent" of profit at the expense of those in need.

Shaking out or off is symbolically significant. The slightly earlier Greek reform of Solon (594–593 B.C.E.), which canceled debts, released slaves, and cut taxes, was called the *Seisachtheia,*[31] literally

---

[30]See chapters 4 and 6, which introduce and follow Nehemiah's debt reform.
[31]Weinfeld, *Social Justice*, 170.

"shaking off a burden" (from the same Greek root that gives us the English word "seismic"). Throughout the ancient world, debt, taxes, forced labor, debt slavery, and national subjugation were described metaphorically as wearing a yoke or carrying a burden.[32] To be liberated from these burdens was to "break or loosen the yoke" and shake it free from your shoulders. This metaphor underlies the use of the word *shemittah* in the deuteronomic debt release legislation (Deut. 15:1–3). At root, it means to loosen and let drop by means of shaking,[33] shaking free from a yoke or binding ropes or fetters, for example. The visual image behind *shemittah* is the image behind the verb *na'ar*, "to shake off" in Nehemiah 5:13 (cf. Isa. 33:9, 15; Ps. 109:23; Judg. 16:20). This narrative does not explicitly mention the law of release, but, by "shaking out" his pockets, Nehemiah symbolically enacts *shemittah* release. He and the wealthy creditors who swear the oath "shake out" the interest debts they hold against needy neighbors and "let them drop."

The word used to describe Nehemiah's symbolic act (*na'ar*, "shake off") is not common in biblical Hebrew, but it is used in a few theologically loaded texts. Exodus 14:27 uses it to describe the victory at the sea: "Yahweh shook off the Egyptians in the midst of the sea!" (cf. Psalm 136:15). In Judges 16:20, Samson mistakenly believes he will "shake off" the fetters of his Philistine captors. In Isaiah 52:2, "captive Jerusalem" is urged to "shake yourself off from the dust and loosen the bonds from your neck." In these texts, "shaking off" metaphorically describes liberation from foreign bondage. Echoes of exodus, exile, and return reverberate in Nehemiah's symbolic act of shaking out his pockets. Like Israel freed from Egyptian, Philistine, and Babylonian lords by the liberating power of Yahweh, the debtors of Israel now have shaken free from bondage to their own greedy kin.

In the broader narrative context of Nehemiah, however, these echoes of sacred history have a threatening edge. The story in chapter 5 is sandwiched between accounts of violent protest against the rebuilding of Jerusalem, hostile conspiracies by local inhabitants who never went into exile. Nehemiah had armed Jewish workers and successfully countered the threat to the rebuilding project. Now in

---

[32]Cf. Gen. 27:40; Lev. 26:13; 1 Kgs. 12:4–14 // 2 Chr. 10:4–14; Isa. 9:4; 10:27; 14:25; 47:6; 58:6, 9; Jer. 27:2–12; 28:2, 10–14; 30:8; Lam. 1:14; 3:27; 5:5; Ezek. 34:27; Nah. 1:13. For further bibliography on debt, taxes, and slavery as a "burden" or "yoke" in ancient Near Eastern literature, Weinfeld, *Social Justice*, 84, n. 38, and 171, n. 69.

[33]Ibid., 170, n. 65.

chapter 5, wealthy "nobles and rulers" within the Jewish community were acting like enemies of Israel, taking interest on subsistence loans and driving fellow Jews into debt slavery. The threat from without had given way to a threat from within. The rich were acting like "foreigners," enemies to their own people. They were playing the role of the Egyptians whom Yahweh "shook off" in the midst of the sea.

The groundwork is laid for this identification at the very beginning of the narrative, by the use of the theologically explosive term "outcry" (*tsa`aqah*). "There was an outcry from the people" (v. 1). In Genesis 4:10, Abel's blood "is crying out" (*tso`eqîm*) to Yahweh from the ground where his own brother had murdered him. Later, Yahweh investigates and finally destroys Sodom and Gomorrah because of the outcry of violent injustice in those prosperous and heartless cities (Gen. 18:21; 19:13; cf. Isa. 1:9–17; Ezek. 16:49). Psalm 9:12 and Job 34:28 lament the outcry of the poor and afflicted. The disappointed gardener in Isaiah's "Song of the Vineyard" (Isa. 5) planted justice (*mishpat*) but got bloodshed (*mispah*), and righteousness (*tsedaqah*) but got an outcry (*tse`aqah*). "Outcry" plays a key role in the exodus narrative. Yahweh commissions Moses to liberate Israel, because "I have seen the oppression of my people who are in Egypt, and I have heard their outcry" (Exod. 3:7; cf. 3:9).[34] 1 Samuel 9:16 alludes to this exodus motif in one of the pro-monarchical versions of Saul's election as king. Yahweh chooses Saul to liberate Israel from Philistine power because God has seen Israel's suffering and "their outcry has come to me."

The most important biblical use of "outcry" for the interpretation of Nehemiah's reform comes in Exodus 22:20–26 [21–27], which addresses unjust treatment of the poor. Verse 20 [21] alludes to the exodus narrative, and verse 22 [23] warns against oppressing the needy, because "when they *cry out* to me, I will certainly listen to their *outcry*. My anger will burn and I will kill you by the sword, so that your wives become widows and your children become orphans!" Verse 24 [25] seals the case against Nehemiah's greedy creditors. "If you lend to my people—that is, the poor of your people—you must not act like a creditor to them. You must not exact interest from them!" If poor debtors *cry out* to me, I will listen" (v. 26 [27]).

---

[34]Yahweh flips Israel's oppression back onto the Egyptians in the plagues, and especially in the final plague of the firstborn. There is "a great outcry" in Egypt the night of Passover (Exod. 11:6; 12:30).

Nehemiah does not specifically appeal to the Hebrew slave law or to debt release to make his case against the creditors. He appeals to common principles of social solidarity and to the culture of honor and shame. But the narrator tells the tale in a way that sets the reform firmly within Israel's larger sacred history. By their greedy profiteering in a time of crisis, the wealthy play the role of pharaoh. If they refuse to "shake off" such ill-gotten gain, Yahweh will "shake them off" from their own inheritance and "empty" them of their prosperity (v. 13).

You Know the Life of the Resident Alien

And a resident alien [we-ger] you must not oppress. You know the life [nefesh] of the resident alien, because you were resident aliens in the land of Egypt. You must plant your land for six years and harvest its produce. But the seventh year, you must release it and leave it alone, so that the needy of your people may eat. What they leave, the living creatures of the field will eat. Do the same with your vineyards and olive orchards. Six days you may do your work, but on the seventh day, you must rest so that your ox and donkey may rest, and your homeborn slave may be revitalized [yinnafesh]—and the resident alien [we-ha-ger]. (Exod. 23:9–12)

This passage appears in the so-called "Book of the Covenant" (Exod. 20:22—23:33), a more or less coherent subsection of laws within the larger book of Exodus that is generally thought to contain the oldest legislation in the Bible.[35] Many of the laws in the Book of the Covenant are similar in form and content to Mesopotamian codes written several centuries before Israel emerged in Canaan. The two laws included in this passage, however, have no clear parallel in known ancient Near Eastern literature outside of the Bible. Their antiquity, therefore, is difficult to judge, except that they probably do not predate Israel. It is also likely—however old these seventh-year and seventh-day laws are—that they had independent origins and only later were linked with one another in the present passage.

Besides sorting out the meaning of the seventh-year law in verses 10–11, the most interesting thing about this passage is the editorial

---

[35]See the discussion of Exodus 21 in the previous chapter.

decision to associate seventh year and seventh day. It is not accidental that these laws appear side by side in Exodus 23. The editor uses the literary technique of "inclusion" to tie these two very different regulations together into a coherent unit. This is achieved by repeating a key word or words at the beginning and end of the unit, to serve as an *inclusio* ("bookends") for the material in between.

The inclusio in this case is composed of two key words, "resident alien" (*ger*) and "life" (*nefesh*). Verse 9 begins, literally in Hebrew, "and a resident alien." Verse 12 ends, with slight syntactical awkwardness, "and the resident alien." Verse 9 warns against oppressing a resident alien because "you know the life [*nefesh*] of the resident alien." Verse 12 says you should rest on the seventh day so "your homeborn slave will be revitalized" (*weyinnafesh*, a verbal form of *nefesh*). The "life" of the "resident alien" is the glue that holds seventh year and seventh day together in this passage.

Reading these laws through the life of the resident alien sets them in the cultural context of social solidarity, among the "universal" norms of conduct that hold ancient Near Eastern communities together. These laws engage those norms at the margins of their reach—at the doorstep of the resident alien, on the very edge of social responsibility to village and clan. But reading these laws through the experience of resident aliens also sets them more specifically within Israel's sacred narrative. There is something about seventh-day rest and seventh-year release that is inexorably bound to liberation from Egypt, where Israel languished as resident aliens and slaves.

The allusion to the exodus story is strengthened by the use, in the first clause, of the verb "to oppress" (*lahats*). The clause reiterates Exodus 22:20 [21], "You must not wrong or oppress a resident alien, because you were resident aliens in Egypt." But more importantly, it alludes to Exodus 3:9, literally in Hebrew, "I have seen the oppressing [*hallahats*] by which the Egyptians are oppressing [*lohetsîm*]" Israel. Oppressing a resident alien runs exactly counter to Israel's sacred history. It associates Israel with the quintessential enemy whom Yahweh defeated so that Israel could live.[36] Israel's identity as God's people and Yahweh's character as the God who liberates slaves are at stake in sabbath and sabbath-year observance.

---

[36]Cf. Judg. 1:34; 2:18; 4:3; 6:9; 10:12; 1 Sam. 10:18; 2 Kgs. 13:4, 22; Isa. 19:20.

It is difficult to know exactly what this seventh-year law requires. The first half of the law (v. 10) is clear: "Six years you will plant your land and you will gather its produce." The proper interpretation of the second half (v. 11)—the heart of the law—is less certain. The ambiguity centers on the precise meaning of the two verbs "release" and "leave alone," and the noun to which their pronouns ("it") refer.

Interpreters traditionally have assumed that the "it" to be "released" and "left alone" in verse 11 refers to "your land" in verse 10. But this is not necessarily the case. Nouns and pronouns in Hebrew have masculine or feminine gender, indicated formally by differences in spelling. Pronouns fit the gender and number of the nouns to which they refer. The pronominal suffix of both verbs in verse 11 is feminine singular. "Land" (*'erets*) in verse 10 is feminine singular, so grammatically "it" in verse 11 may refer to "your land" in verse 10. But "produce" (*tebû'ah*) is also feminine singular. "It" in verse 11 could just as easily refer to "produce" as to "land" in verse 10: "Release [its produce] and leave it alone." In other words, this law may be focusing on the product rather than the process of agriculture. The issue may not be whether the land is planted—as suggested by the translation "let it rest and lie fallow"—but who controls the produce at harvest time—as suggested by the rationale that follows the command. You must "release it" and "leave it alone," "so that the poor of your people may eat" (v. 11). The question is who controls and consumes the harvest—"you" or "the poor of your people"? The seventh year differs from the other six, not because land is left unfarmed, but because "you" do not "gather its produce" for your own use. The seventh-year law is about distribution, not production.

The verbs "release" and "leave alone" also give rise to ambiguity. "Release it" is a verbal form of the noun *shemittah* ("release") in Deuteronomy 15, literally "to loosen" or "let drop." In the context of debt release in Deuteronomy 15, it means to give up control of a loan you have made to someone, to "loosen your grip," to relinquish your power to collect payment. In Exodus 23:11, "you" are called to relinquish your power over "it": "Release it!" The second verb, "leave it alone" (*netashettahh*), means "to abandon" or "leave." Interpreters traditionally have understood this verb to mean "let lie fallow"—a meaning for this verb peculiar to this verse and derived from the literary context here. This translation is rooted in the assumption that "it" refers to "your land" rather than "its produce" in verse 10. To "leave the land alone" is to forego agriculture, to let the land "lie fallow."

Interpreters also derive this meaning for the verb here by reading the Priestly sabbath-year legislation (Lev. 25:2–7) into it. The two laws begin roughly the same way: "Six years you will plant your field and six years you will prune your vineyard and gather its produce" (Lev. 25:3), and "six years you will plant your land and gather its produce" (Exod. 23:10). But the purposes of the laws are completely different. Exodus urges release, "so the poor of your people may eat." Leviticus makes no mention of the needy. Leviticus 25:4–5 clearly, if incredibly, advocates completely stopping agriculture for a year: "The seventh year will be a sabbath of complete rest (*shabbat shabbatôn*) for the land, a sabbath for Yahweh. You will not plant your field or prune your vineyard. You will not reap the aftergrowth of your harvest or cut the grapes of your unpruned vine." Sabbath year clearly is a fallow year, a year of complete rest for the land. Different purposes in Leviticus and Exodus may require different procedures.

It is interesting that Exodus 23 makes no effort to address the practical impact of the seventh-year law and potential objections to observing it, as Deuteronomy 15 and Leviticus 25 do.[37] In Exodus 23, "releasing" and "abandoning" require no more comment than "honor your father and mother" or "do not murder" do. Observing seventh-year law apparently does not carry the same potential for disruption that deuteronomic debt release and Priestly sabbath year do.

It is possible that "releasing" and "abandoning" is not required for every field all at once. Perhaps the law envisions some kind of rotation, an ancient "set aside" program, in which some but not all fields are designated each year on a seven-year cycle for the ongoing economic support of the poor. Such a rotation makes practical sense of a law that otherwise is difficult to fathom. It is not clear how a nationwide ban on agriculture every seven years would benefit the poor—other than perhaps giving them the cruel pleasure of seeing everybody else starve too. Even if they were allowed to feast on the seventh-year harvest, what would they do the other six years? The "feast or famine" cycle fostered by such a law would leave the poor

---

[37]Deuteronomy 15:9–11 threatens moral sanctions against creditors who refuse to loan money in the sixth year. Leviticus 25:18–22 promises a miraculous triple yield every sixth year to make up for the losses caused by abandoning agriculture in the seventh year. Leviticus 26:34–35 promises (after the event) that Israel will be exiled from the land for failure to observe sabbath year.

destitute for most of their short, brutish lives. But relinquishing produce of set-aside fields and vineyards every year on a seven-year rotation would provide ongoing relief for the poor without leading to periodic starvation among the non-poor completely cut off from their harvests every seventh year.

If indeed the seventh-year law in Exodus 23 is a "set aside" program on a seven-year rotation, it is more closely akin to the gleaning tradition and the deuteronomic triennial tithe than to the sabbath-year law in Leviticus 25. According to Leviticus 19:9–10, 23:22, and Deuteronomy 24:19–21 (cf. Ruth 2), the poor have a moral claim on part of the harvest of every field, vineyard, and olive orchard. Deuteronomy 14:28–29, the passage immediately before the debt-release law, requires that a tithe of the harvest be set aside every three years for the Levite, the widow, and the orphan. Seventh year in Exodus 23 is an extension of the principle of mutual support that underlies these laws. Or, more precisely, it is the way the book of Exodus enacts the principle of social solidarity and ongoing care for the poor.

Summary

Deuteronomic debt release is similar in content to proclamations of liberty decreed when a new king took the throne or conquered new territories. The deuteronomic law is exceptional in the ancient world because it fixes debt release in a seven-year cycle nationwide. Deuteronomic release distinguishes between debts owed by "neighbors," which are canceled in the seventh year, and those owed by "foreigners," which are not. The distinction is not primarily ethnic, however. Loans to "neighbors" are subsistence loans made to clan households and affiliated resident aliens. Loans to "foreigners" are commercial loans related to trade.

Jeremiah 34 blames Babylonian exile on an aborted release during the reign of the last Davidic king, Zedekiah. The historical veracity of this unique account is questionable. It conflates the slave and debt laws of Deuteronomy and the jubilee tradition of Leviticus 25 and is noteworthy for arguing that slavery should be abolished in Israel—a step beyond the Hebrew slave laws in Exodus and Deuteronomy.

Nehemiah's case against wealthy creditors of Jerusalem is prompted by the "outcry" of debtors. Nehemiah's solution focuses on the evil of charging interest on subsistence loans. The story makes several allusions to Israel's sacred narrative of liberation from various human oppressors, but especially the Egyptians. Rhetorically, Nehemiah casts the wealthy creditors of Jerusalem in the frightening role of the pharaoh. Those who exploit the weakness of the poor are on the losing side of sacred history.

Finally, Exodus 23 ties seventh-day rest to seventh-year release. Both are intended to help the vulnerable, especially to "preserve the life" of the "resident alien." The precise meaning of the seventh-year law in this passage is uncertain. Traditionally understood to require periodic fallowing of fields and vineyards, the critical verse 11 is unclear. It may well be "produce" and not "land" that must be "released" and "abandoned" in the seventh year, since the purpose is to feed the poor and animals of the field. The seven-year cycle may be a seven-year rotation in which selected fields are "set aside" each year for the ongoing support of the poor. Seventh-year release in Exodus 23 is related to gleaning traditions and the deuteronomic triennial tithe for the poor.

All these passages connect economic justice and support for the vulnerable with Israel's sacred narrative of liberation. Greedy profiteers play the role of the pharaoh and other finally vanquished enemies of Israel. Those who help the vulnerable and resist injustice stand with Yahweh, the redeemer and liberator of slaves.

5

PROCLAIM LIBERTY!

Leviticus 25 first identifies the seventh year as "sabbath" year. Though largely impractical as real-world social policy, the sabbath-year and jubilee traditions lay theological and ethical foundations for revolutionary change. Ironically, these most utopian of the seventh-year traditions hold special promise for a modern theological ethic of economic justice and ecological care. This chapter focuses on sabbath year and jubilee in Leviticus 25—26 and related texts in Nehemiah 10, 1 Maccabees 6, and Isaiah 60—61.

Leviticus 25—26

The Priestly sabbath-year and jubilee laws are set within the "Holiness Code," a very large section of Leviticus that begins in chapter 17 and runs through the end of the book. Though some of its laws and customs certainly date from an earlier period, the Holiness Code is late exilic (mid to late 500s) at the earliest.

The sabbath-year and jubilee laws form a coherent literary unit within the Holiness Code. Chapters 25 and 26 are uninterrupted and continuous, without noticeable redactional seams or shifts in voice or setting. Though the laws in these chapters give evidence of growth

57

over time, the chapters themselves do not appear to be products of multiple sources.

An intriguing inclusion sets sabbath-year and jubilee laws in chapters 25—26 apart from their immediate literary context and outside the narrative setting of most of the rest of the book. Sabbath-year and jubilee laws were given "at Mount Sinai" (25:1; 26:46). The book's introductory superscription establishes the narrative setting of law-giving in Leviticus as "the tent of meeting" (1:1). This is the implied and often explicit narrative setting for lawgiving through most of the book. The only exceptions come at the end of the sacrificial laws (7:38), at the end of the chapter 27 addendum to the book (27:34), and in the inclusion that introduces and concludes sabbath-year and jubilee laws in chapters 25—26. Chapter 27 builds on jubilee laws in chapters 25—26 and repeats their narrative setting. That leaves 7:38 as the only other Sinai setting in Leviticus. The extraordinary setting of sabbath-year and jubilee laws "at Mount Sinai" not only establishes the literary coherency of chapters 25—26 as a distinct unit in Leviticus but also connects sabbath year and jubilee with the sacrificial legislation that introduces the Leviticus scroll (chapters 1—7).

A Sabbath for the Land

Then Yahweh spoke to Moses on Mount Sinai: "Speak to the Israelites and say to them, 'When you come to the land that I am giving you, the land will rest, a sabbath for Yahweh. Six years you will plant your field and six years you will prune your vineyard and gather its produce. But in the seventh year, it will be a sabbath of complete rest (*shabbat shabbatôn*) for the land, a sabbath for Yahweh. You must not plant your field or prune your vineyard. You must not harvest what comes up volunteer from your [previous] harvest, and you must not cut the grapes from your untrimmed vines. It will be a year of complete rest (*shabbatôn*) for the land. The sabbath of the land will be food for you all—for you, for your male slave, your female slave, your hired worker, your guest worker, the resident aliens among you, your beasts, and the creatures in your land—all its produce will be food.'" (Lev. 25:1–7)

But if you say, "What will we eat in the seventh year if we are not allowed to plant or to harvest our produce?" I will order my blessing for you in the sixth year. The produce will yield enough for three years. You will plant the eighth year and eat from the old produce until the ninth year—until its produce comes, you will eat the old. The land will not be permanently sold, because the land is mine, because you are resident aliens and guest workers with me. So in all the land you hold, you must provide the right of redemption for the land." (Lev. 25:20–24)

Then the land will enjoy its sabbaths, through all the days of desolation with you in the land of your enemies—then the land will rest and enjoy its sabbaths...it will rest as it did not rest during your sabbaths when you were living on it. (Lev. 26:34–35)

Sabbath year in Leviticus 25 is a utopian vision of the world that has much more in common with the Priestly creation-sabbath and sabbath-manna stories in Genesis 1 and Exodus 16 than with genuine social reforms proposed in the seventh-year laws of Deuteronomy 15 and Exodus 23.

It is hard to know exactly what this law has in mind. It is clear, however, that sabbath year would be utterly impractical for Israel through most of the biblical period. If it were fully implemented, it would lead to mass starvation. Unlike Exodus 23, which sets aside the produce of fields and vineyards on a seven-year rotation for the ongoing support of the poor, the sabbath year law in Leviticus calls for a complete cessation of agriculture, a total ban on planting and harvesting for an entire year every seven years. Verse 5 even forbids gathering fruit and grain that grow up without planting or pruning, the volunteer aftergrowth of the sixth year's harvest. Sabbath year pulls the plug on an entire mode of production. For two years every seven years, agrarian Israel must become a society of hunters and gatherers, with these two qualifications: They may eat agricultural product stored from previous harvests, and they must not gather fruits, vegetables, and grains that grow as the unintended result of agriculture in previous years.

The meaning of verse 6 is uncertain, but it seems to say that observance itself will provide necessary sustenance in the seventh year: "The sabbath year will be food for you all...all its produce will be food." Let them eat sabbath year! NRSV handles the obvious problem posed by the literal translation by translating verse 6 in light of the jubilee law in verses 11–12: "You will not plant or harvest its aftergrowth or cut its unpruned vines... From the field, you may eat its produce." According to NRSV's translation of verse 6: "You may eat what the land yields during its sabbath"—that is, you can eat whatever grows up of its own accord. This free translation makes sense of the concluding clause of verse 7, "all its produce will be food." But it risks contradicting verse 5, which unambiguously bans the harvesting of fruits and grains that spring up of their own accord during this year of complete rest for the land. In verse 5, the issue is not planting, but harvesting. The people may not consume anything that grows as the intended or unintended result of agriculture or horticulture because, during its sabbath, the land is freed from all work for Israel—even leftover work from the previous year.

Verses 20–22 anticipate popular panic at the very idea of sabbath year: "What will we eat in the seventh year if we are not allowed to plant or gather our produce?" In response, Yahweh promises a triple harvest in the sixth year, enough to last until the crop planted in the eighth year is harvested at the beginning of the ninth.[1] Until the harvest of the eighth year's planting, "you will eat the old," that is, the remainder of the sixth-year harvest, stored for the last two years. This seems to assume that no fresh food will be gathered for two full years. The entire nation will survive on crops in storage.

Even in the unlikely event of a triple harvest one year, it is difficult to imagine how an entire agrarian population could survive for two years on stored grains and fruit, supplemented only by things that grow completely wild. This would be impossible in the modern world, with our historically unparalleled ability to produce and store agricultural produce. It is unthinkable that an entire nation in the ancient world could live for two years on stored food.

The Roman-era Jewish historian Josephus says, however, that Jews in Judea in the Hellenistic and Roman periods observed an agricultural sabbath year.[2] But Judea in Josephus' day was much more urban and multicultural than Judah was in the earlier biblical period. The trade economy was more established. Non-Jews shared the land and farmed it. It is within the realm of possibility that wealthy Judeans

---

[1] The calendar year begins at fall harvest in this reckoning; the spring planting in the eighth year is harvested that fall, the beginning of the ninth.

[2] Flavius Josephus, *The Antiquities of the Jews,* XI.8.6; XIII.8.1; XIV.10. 6; XV.1.2; *The Wars of the Jews or the History of the Destruction of Jerusalem,* I.2.4.

and city dwellers employed in nonagrarian occupations were able to buy agricultural produce from non-Jewish neighbors and to import enough food to survive for a year without the income of rural estates. But it is unthinkable that even in Josephus' day everyone in Judea would stop planting, pruning, and harvesting for a year. Josephus' comments, if historically accurate, more likely apply to urban elites who forfeited some or all the produce of their estates in the seventh year for the sake of the poor, along the lines of the release in Exodus 23.

Commentators often observe that sabbath year in Leviticus does not provide for the poor, as seventh-year laws in Exodus 23 and Deuteronomy 15 do. They note that such provisions are made in the jubilee legislation that follows in Leviticus 25. What interpreters seldom say is that sabbath year, as Leviticus 25 sets it up, is utopian. Debt release in Deuteronomy 15 and crop set-aside in Exodus 23 put challenging limits on economic business-as-usual, but they are at least within the realm of possibility. Sabbath year in Leviticus 25, if universally applied in the land, would lead to mass starvation. It is impractical.

The sabbath-year law, however, does not promise practical results. The point is not to give sustenance to the poor or to increase the agricultural productivity of the land by letting it lie fallow. Indeed, a seven-year fallow cycle is not frequent enough. A two- or three-year cycle would be more fitting to the soil structure and climate of ancient Palestine. Sabbath year is not "responsible farming." It is public affirmation of the land's freedom under Yahweh's sovereign rule. Like sabbath-day rest for "your ox and your donkey, your homeborn slave and the resident alien" (Exod. 23:12), sabbath year is the land's rest from work for Israel.

Sabbath year, like the creation-sabbath narrative in Genesis 1, rejects an overly anthropocentric view of the world. Human beings, as Genesis 1:26–28 portrays them, are rulers of creation. But God establishes the value of creation long before human beings enter the picture. In the sabbath-year law as well, the land is worthwhile in its own right, apart from its usefulness to human beings. The land has its own justice, enforced by Yahweh, that cannot be overridden by human needs and wants.

In Leviticus 25:23, Yahweh asserts personal ownership of the land, as Yahweh later asserts for Israel, bought as slaves (25:42) from Egypt. This idea of Yahweh's ownership of land and people connects both with the exodus narratives, particularly with rhetoric that describes Yahweh as the "redeemer" (Exod. 6:6; 15:13) who buys Israel out of debt slavery. Sabbath year underlines that the land, like the people who occupy it, is redeemed—bought and owned by Yahweh. As Israel's liberation from Egypt expresses the character of Yahweh, so too the people's respect for the land in sabbath year honors God.

Yahweh's ownership of land and people has practical implications. As we saw previously, dedicating a people to the servitude of a god freed them from human bondage. Having been bought as slaves of Yahweh (Lev. 25:42), Israel is forever freed from human slavery. Likewise, by owning the land, Yahweh frees it from bondage to human beings. The principle by which slavery is abolished for Israelites in Leviticus 25:42 begins with the land itself. Owned by Yahweh, the land is liberated from human bondage. The earth has its own vocation to obey and worship God and its own worth apart from its usefulness to human beings. The land exists in relationship with human society as a partner, not an objectified commodity to be exploited without limit. To borrow the language of the twentieth-century philosopher Martin Buber, sabbath year establishes that the land is a "Thou," not an "It."

The I-Thou relationship between people and land is so important that the people must pay the price of exile for violating the land's integrity. In one of the most amazing passages of the Bible, Leviticus 26:34–35 interprets Babylonian exile as punishment for Israel's theft of the land's sabbath years. Failure to respect the integrity of the earth is the moral equivalent of kidnaping or murder. It is, for Israel, a capital crime.

Sabbath Year and Sabbath

Sabbath year in Leviticus 25 is closely related to sabbath-day narratives in Genesis 1 and Exodus 16. All three texts share Priestly authorship,[3] and Leviticus 25 explicitly connects seventh year with sabbath, describing it as a "sabbath of complete rest" (*shabbat shabbatôn*).

The miraculous triple harvest of the sixth year in Leviticus' sabbath-year law resonates with utopian visions of abundance in the

---

[3]A Priestly redactor has supplemented and edited older material from the Yahwist (J) in the sabbath-manna story in Exodus 16.

sabbath-creation and sabbath-manna stories. In Genesis 1, the world as God intended it is a world of overflowing abundance, shared power, self-restraint, and universal leisure. It is the opposite of life actually experienced by peasant farmers under ancient Near Eastern monarchies, where taxes, debt, and the uncertainties of nature left households chronically overworked and on the brink of economic disaster. But creation-sabbath in Genesis 1:1—2:4a promises prosperity that exceeds the work put into producing it, a superabundance of wealth and well-being that allows everyone to take a weekly rest from the struggle to survive. In Exodus 16, Yahweh promises a double harvest of manna every sixth day. Though manna normally could not be stored overnight, God preserves the sixth day's double harvest so that the people can refrain from work on sabbath. In Leviticus, Israel can observe sabbath year because Yahweh provides miraculous sixth-year harvest and three-year storage. Sabbath day and sabbath year are thematically connnected and properly read through the same theological lens.

Foregoing the Debt

> When the people of the land bring in merchandise or any grain on the sabbath day to sell, we will not buy from them on the sabbath or on a holy day. We also will forego [*we-nittosh*] the seventh year and the exaction of any debt. (Neh. 10:32 [31])

Like Leviticus 25 and Exodus 23, this passage links sabbath day and sabbath year. This is further evidence that, though seventh-year laws developed independently of one another and of sabbath, seventh-year and seventh-day observance came to be associated, certainly by the late biblical period. It is also notable that some English translations link this verse with agricultural sabbath year in Leviticus 25 and Exodus 23.

RSV and NRSV translate *we-nittosh* as "and we will forego the crops." But this offers a misleading picture of what the people actually agreed to do. The root word *natash* means "to leave alone," "to relinquish power over." In Exodus 23, it appears in parallelism with a form of the verb *shamat*, "release" (cf. *shemittah*), and means to give up control of agricultural produce, to turn it over to the poor for their consumption. Here in Nehemiah 10, it also means to relinquish power and control. But the rest of the verse suggests that what is relinquished is the power to collect on debt: literally, "we will forego the seventh year and the exaction of any debt." The two parts of this sentence are parallel. They describe one action, not two. "Foregoing" the seventh year means forfeiting the right to collect a debt. The people are making a covenant to observe debt release (*shemittah*).

Sabbath-Year Defeat

> The soldiers of the king's army went up to Jerusalem against [the Jews], and the king encamped in Judea and at Mount Zion. He made peace with the people of Beth-zur, and they evacuated the town because they had no provisions there to withstand a siege, since it was a sabbatical year for the land… Then he encamped before the sanctuary [at Jerusalem] for many days…The Jews… fought for many days. But they had no food in storage, because it was the seventh year; those who had found safety in Judea from the Gentiles had consumed the last of the stores. Only a few men were left in the sanctuary; the rest scattered to their own homes, for the famine proved too much for them. (1 Macc. 6:48–54, NRSV)

At first reading, this passage appears to support sabbath-year observance along the lines of Leviticus 25. First, the city of Beth-zur is forced to surrender to the imperial army because the people there had no provisions to withstand a siege, "since it was a sabbatical year for the land." Then most of the men defending Jerusalem flee the sanctuary under the pressure of siege, since "they had no food in storage, because it was the seventh year," and those who had fled the Gentile army had consumed the last of the stored crops. It is plausible to interpret these passages in light of the sabbath-year law in Leviticus 25.[4] The people are attempting to live for two years on the stored harvest of the sixth year. The resulting famine makes them unable to resist the imperial army.

The response of Jerusalem's defenders to the siege-induced famine, however, speaks against this interpretation. A "skeleton crew" remains in the temple, while "the rest scattered to their own homes, for the famine proved too much." The problem is not access to food anywhere in the land, but the size of the food reserve inside the city.

---

[4]This is certainly the way Josephus reads it (*Ant.*, XIV.16.2).

The siege has cut off Beth-zur's and Jerusalem's access to crops from surrounding farmlands. They must rely on food stores inside the city walls. The combination of sabbath-year shortage and military siege has drained the stores inside the city—exactly the point of a siege. So the defenders flee to their homes outside the city walls to escape the famine caused by siege. Food apparently is available in the country-side even though it is a sabbath year.

One way to explain the facts of the narrative is to assume that the seventh-year observance that leaves the cities short on supplies is not the sabbath year of Leviticus 25, but something more along the lines of release in Exodus 23 and Deuteronomy 15. City-dwelling estate owners have relinquished their right to collect debts, tax property, and extract produce from indebted farms and prebendal estates outside the city during the seventh year. They have canceled rent and loan payments for a year. So food stores inside the city walls are low, making it impossible for them to withstand a prolonged siege. If this interpretation is right, the story in 1 Maccabees supports the idea that Jews actually did observe a seventh-year release for the economic support of the poor. In this case, their social commitment left them vulnerable.

A Jubilee for You!

> You will count seven sabbath years, seven years times seven. The period of seven sabbath years will give you forty-nine years. You must sound a blast on the trumpet in the seventh month on the tenth of the month, on the day of atonement— you must sound the trumpet through all your land. You must keep the fiftieth year holy, and you must declare liberty [derôr] in the land for all its inhabitants. It will be a jubilee[yôbel] for you. You will each return to your property, and you will each return to your clan. The fiftieth year will be a jubilee for you. You must not sow or harvest its aftergrowth and you must not cut from its unpruned vines. For it is jubilee. It will be holy to you. From the field you may eat its produce. In this year of jubilee you will each return to your property. (Lev. 25:8–13)

Several questions surround the jubilee legislation. Does jubilee start at the beginning of the forty-ninth year or at the end? If jubilee begins at the end of the forty-ninth year, a sabbath year, is Israel required to observe sabbath year in the months leading up to jubilee? Observing jubilee right after sabbath year would require the entire nation to take a two-year vacation from planting crops and a three-year break from harvesting! As we asked in the section on sabbath year, what does it mean to eat the produce of the field during jubilee, if you are not allowed to harvest the aftergrowth of previous years' planting or the fruit that grows from unpruned vines? How could Israel possibly survive an agricultural sabbath year followed immediately by jubilee? Finally, what does it mean for debt slaves to return to their clans and ancestral property every fifty years, since Leviticus 25 appears to abolish debt slavery?

Some of these questions cannot be answered definitively. This is true in part because the sabbath-year and jubilee traditions are complicated and thoroughly interspersed in Leviticus 25. It is hard to know how to sort them out. The text bears the marks of a fluid past, swirling back and forth between sabbath, sabbath year, and jubilee and from one jubilee tradition to another. It gives the impression of a work in progress, an unfolding Priestly reflection on life in a land structured by jubilee. It moves from rest for the land to respite for the poor, protection for the vulnerable, restoration for the dislocated, and freedom for the enslaved. It sets prices for land transactions and terms for subsistence loans. It provides support for the poor and recovers ancestral property lost through the economic pressures of ancient monarchies. And, except in jubilee's implications for property values, jubilee laws, to the extent that they could ever be enacted, would have had little practical impact—except once in a lifetime, when they would have turned national life completely upside down.

Rabbis in the Second Temple period apparently thought that jubilee had not been operative for quite some time. Talmudic discussions of sabbath year and jubilee indicate that neither set of practices had the authority of biblical law after the fall of the Davidic monarchy, or even before the exile of 586 B.C.E. The key to this interpretation is the proclamation of jubilee liberty to "all the inhabitants in the land" (Lev. 25:10). The diaspora (the "scattering" of Jews outside the land of Israel) made jubilee and sabbath-year observance impossible, since "all" of Israel no longer lived "in the land." But Israel's scattering began before 586 B.C.E. As medieval commentator Moses Maimonides argues, "Since the tribes of Reuven and Gad and half the tribe of Menasheh were exiled [cf. Num. 32; Deut. 3:8–22; Josh. 12:6;13:8], the jubilees were canceled. As it says, 'Proclaim liberty in the land to all of its inhabitants' (Lev. 25:10), i.e., at a time when all of [the land's] inhabitants are in it."[5] Some elements of sabbath year and jubilee—those related to debt release—were observed during the second temple period under rabbinical authority as moral instruction, so Israel would not forget jubilee and sabbath year, though they were no longer binding as biblical law. As Maimonides says, "In accordance with the words of the Scribes, the release of debts is operative at this time in every place, although the Jubilee is not operative, so that the Torah of release of debts might not be forgotten in Israel."[6]

Though jubilee may not have been observed as an ongoing obligation in Israel, some of the specific practices of jubilee are plausible as social policy in the ancient world. Jubilee year is a liberty (*derôr*) declared through the whole land, according to verse 10. As we saw in the last chapter, canceling debts, freeing slaves, and returning ancestral property were common in the ancient world when a new king took the throne. In fact, viewed against some of the more extensive royal reforms in the ancient world, the measures advocated by the jubilee laws are relatively tame—though their universal scope in Israel is striking.

Jubilee liberty has three components: completely stopping agriculture, restoring ancestral property, and returning (from debt slavery) to one's clan of birth. Completely stopping agriculture for a year repeats the core requirement of the sabbath-year law, an impractical program that would be disastrous if enforced as actual social policy nationwide. To do it one year would be suicidal. To do it two years in a row—sabbath year 49 and jubilee year 50—would be impossible, since everyone would be dead.

Releasing debt slaves to return to their clans, on the other hand, has value as actual social policy. But, since 25:35–55 abolishes slavery for Israelites, it has no practical consequence. Verses 35–43 explicitly forbid treating Jewish debt slaves as debt slaves. Verse 39 sums it up this way: "If your kin with you become so impoverished that they sell themselves to you, you must not make them serve as slaves." Verses 42 and 55 assert Yahweh's exclusive ownership of all Israelites,

---

[5]Maimonides, *Mishneh Torah*, Hilkhot Shemittah ve-Yovel 10:8. Cited by Raphael Jospe, "Sabbath, Sabbatical and Jubilee: Jewish Ethical Perspectives," *The Jubilee Challenge: Utopia or Possibility? Jewish and Christian Insights*, ed. Hans Ucko (Geneva: WCC Publications, 1997), 91–92.

[6]Ibid., 9:3. Cited by Jospe, *Jubilee Challenge*, 92.

effectively liberating them from enslavement to any human master. The jubilee legislation envisions total abolition of slavery for Jews. In this regard, it is much more radical than the Hebrew slave law in Exodus 21 and Deuteronomy 15, which only seek to limit the term and consequences of debt servitude. What does it mean then to allow the poor, taken in as household wards, to return to their own clans and ancestral property in the year of jubilee (vv. 10, 41)? Can people who are not enslaved be liberated? Verse 35 requires that economically secure households must provide support to the poor—no slave strings attached! Under these circumstances, poor families might be better off living in the households of the rich than returning to their clans and ancestral property during jubilee. In any case, it is difficult to imagine how a non-slave slave release every fifty years would be of much practical use to people who had an average life span of forty years. Practically speaking, the six-year Hebrew slave law of Exodus 21 and Deuteronomy 15 is a much better deal for the slave.

Of the three legs of jubilee reform, only the restoration of ancestral property makes sense as an actual social reform. But serious questions remain about how practical such a massive redistribution of land would be as regular social policy. And no evidence exists that its observation was actually an ongoing practice.

A fifty-year redistribution of land would benefit households through time but provide no immediate relief for individuals who fall into economic difficulty. With a forty-year life span, chances are that the householder who lost ancestral property would never live to see it returned in jubilee. But relief for the individual poor is not the point of this legislation. The long-term survival of households and preservation of ancestral property are at stake in jubilee land redistribution. Jubilee observance, though effectively outside the life span of individual Israelites, would serve as a check on the long-term concentration of wealth in the hands of a rich few.

However impractical, jubilee land redistribution is a systemic solution to a systemic problem of royal political economy: the persistent inability of subsistence farmers to meet royal obligations and survive without losing the family farm. Jubilee is not rapid response to an immediate need, a social safety net for the individual poor. Individual families may win or lose as a result of land redistribution. Jubilee addresses broad economic trends that undermine families over time. It critiques and seeks to correct fundamental flaws in the ancient royal political economy. Jubilee is economic revolution, not charity.

There is no evidence that jubilee was observed, but there is a time when jubilee land redistribution would have made political sense. In 538 B.C.E., after roughly fifty years of Babylonian exile, the children and grandchildren of royal priests and bureaucrats who had been deported from Jerusalem in 597 and 586 B.C.E. were allowed by Persian imperial edict to return to Judah to rebuild Jerusalem and its temple. Though biblical narratives tend to portray the second deportation in 586 as a nearly total emptying of the land, a more careful reading suggests that only social elites associated with the Davidic monarchy and its royal cult were exiled to Babylonia. The politically insignificant majority stayed in Judah. When the Persian king Cyrus conquered Babylon, he declared liberty for Judeans exiled to Babylonia and offered imperial support for the rebuilding of Jerusalem (2 Chr. 36:22–23//Ezra 1:1–3a). Temple building and repair in the ancient Near East made a political statement, expressing the local deity's support for the royal patron who built the temple (2 Sam. 7:1–17; 1 Kgs. 5:2–5; 8:22–26). By supporting the efforts of returning exiles to rebuild Jerusalem, Cyrus strengthened his political claim on Judah.

The Persian-supported exiles returned to a land long inhabited by Judeans too insignificant to deport. Land disputes were inevitable. Jubilee would settle many of those disputes in favor of returning exiles, as well as provide some relief to households who had stayed in the land and fallen prey to Babylonian, Samaritan, and native creditors.[7] Tearing up all the deeds in Judah and returning every plot to the household that owned it fifty years ago was an effective way to handle legal complications of repatriating a displaced population after fifty years of absence. Such a solution may not have sat well with the occupants, but returning exiles had the backing of the Persian Empire, which now controlled the land. Even if such a jubilee were enforced at the end of the exile, however, it apparently did not become a permanent feature of life in Judah.

In some ways, the most interesting and enduring aspects of the jubilee law in Leviticus 25 take place outside of jubilee year itself. The

---

[7]Norman K. Gottwald, "The Biblical Jubilee: In Whose Interests?" In *Jubilee Challenge*, 36–38.

underlying notion that Yahweh owns both land and people reorients economic assumptions and lays the moral foundation of a just society. Land is not a commodity to be bought and sold. Purchasers buy only the produce that grows from jubilee to jubilee. This principle not only sets a minimum price for household property when it must be sold, it also implies that there are limits to what human "owners" can do with the land that they control. As the property of Yahweh, the land answers finally to God. It serves God by blessing Israel, whom Yahweh has redeemed. And God, not the human "owner," sets the terms of the land's use. The same principle applies to Israel's poor. Their vulnerable condition does not justify treating them or their labor as commodities to be exploited without limit. As slaves of Yahweh, they are slaves to no human master. They must be treated with the same respect due to God. Land and people are Yahweh's possessions and, therefore, inherently worthy of honor and free from human domination. This principle is expressed where the jubilee law reiterates the ban on interest lending (25:36–37) and issues extensive rules about care for the poor (25:35–43) and redemption of Israelite property and persons lost through debt foreclosure and sale (25:25–34, 47–55). It is clearest in the abolition of Israelite slavery (25:39–42, 55). Though very different than seventh-year laws in Exodus and Deuteronomy, the underlying principles of jubilee express the same sense of social solidarity that gave rise to slave release, debt release, gleaning, and other means of relief for the poor.

The jubilee laws, like sabbath-year law in Leviticus, are important, not for the practical impact of their actual observance, but for the theological and moral principles that they establish. Though these laws do not advocate universal abolition of slavery, for example, they do establish the principle that Yahweh's people are inherently free, that slavery is an affront to God's relationship with Israel. Paired with the more universal vision of literary contemporaries, such as the author of Isaiah 56, the jubilee ban on Israelite slavery lays the moral foundation for the universal abolition of human slavery. "'My house will be a house of prayer for all peoples,' says Yahweh my lord who gathers the outcasts of Israel, 'I will gather others to them besides the ones already gathered!'" (Isa. 56:7–8).

Jubilee is tied to the larger theological narrative of Israel in a number of ways. But one of the most powerful, if subtle, connections comes with the announcement of jubilee: "You must sound a blast on the trumpet (*shofar*) in the seventh month on the tenth of the month, on the Day of Atonement" (25:9). Jubilee begins on the Day of Atonement (cf. Lev. 16:1–34; Num. 29:7–11), which Leviticus 23 places just after the "festival of trumpets" (23:23–32; Num. 29:1–11). The Day of Atonement, like sabbath year and jubilee, is a sabbath of complete rest (*shabbatôn*, 16:29–31; 23:28–32; Num. 29:7), a day of self-denial (16:29; 23:27; Num. 29:7). Most importantly, it is a day of purification for the people and the sanctuary (16:1–34) to prepare Israel to stand in the royal presence of Yahweh, who appears "in the cloud over the mercy seat" (16:2). Announced on the Day of Atonement, jubilee is associated with Israel's purification, its holiness. Jubilee prepares Israel to encounter God.

Jubilee liberty is announced by trumpet blast. In Torah and Prophets, blowing the trumpet usually signals the beginning or end of battle[8] and the election or coronation of a king.[9] In the psalms, the trumpet blast is associated with Yahweh's royal enthronement as king of the universe and liberator of Israel (Pss. 47:6 [5]; 81:4 [3]; 98:6; 150:3). The trumpet's associations with human and divine coronation merge when David brings the ark of the covenant into his new capital city. David leads the procession, dancing before the ark with trumpet blasts and the sound of the *shofar* (2 Sam. 6:15//1 Chr. 15:28; cf. Isa. 27:13). Leviticus 23:24–25 and Numbers 29:1–6 describe a festival of trumpets or "day of acclamation" (Num. 29:1) for Yahweh just before the Day of Atonement, possibly celebrating Yahweh as lord of the agricultural cycle. Numbers 10:1–10 instructs Aaronid priests to blow trumpets for various reasons related to Yahweh's cult—alarms, convocations, new moons, burnt offerings, and sacrifices.

In Israel's encounter with Yahweh at Mount Sinai in Exodus 19—20, God appears to Israel and Moses with thunder and lightning and "a trumpet blast so loud that all the people in the camp trembled" (19:16; cf. 20:18). As the trumpet blasts grow louder, Moses speaks and Yahweh answers in thunder (19:19). The blowing of the *shofar,* the trumpet, signals theophany—specifically, the people's encounter with God at Mount Sinai. This connection is made explicit in the jubilee tradition by the extraordinary literary inclusion that introduces

---

[8]Josh. 6:4–6, 8–9, 13, 16, 20; Judg. 3:27; 7:8, 16, 18–20, 22; 1 Sam. 13:3; 2 Sam. 2:28; 18:16; 20:1, 22; Isa. 18:3; 58:1; Jer. 4:5, 19, 21; 6:1, 17; 51:27; Ezek. 33:3–6; Hos. 5:8; 8:1; Joel 2:1; Amos 2:2; 3:6; Zeph. 1:16; Zech. 9:14; cf. Job 39:24–25; Neh. 4:12 [18], 14 [20].
[9]2 Sam. 15:10; 1 Kgs. 1:34, 39, 41; 2 Kgs. 9:13; cf. Asa's reform in 2 Chr. 15:14.

and concludes the jubilee laws in Leviticus 25—26: "Yahweh spoke to Moses on Mount Sinai" (25:1; 26:46).

Jubilee observance, announced with trumpet blast on the Day of Atonement, is a Sinai experience for Israel, a direct encounter with the God who redeems and frees them from all human bondage. The social legislation associated with jubilee—abolishing slavery and usury, redistributing land, allowing the land to rest—reveals Yahweh. When Israel exercises jubilee self-restraint for the sake of the poor and the well-being of the land, they purify and prepare themselves. In these acts of mercy and justice, Israel encounters God.

God Will Stroll Among You

You must not make yourselves idols. You must not set up an image or pillar for yourself. Nor may you put figured stone in your land to worship at it, because I am Yahweh your God! My sabbaths you must keep, my sanctuary you must revere, because I am Yahweh! If you walk in my statutes and keep my commandments and do them, then I will give your rain in its appropriate time so that the earth will yield its produce and the tree of the field will yield its fruit. Your threshing will overtake the vintage, and the vintage will overtake the planting, and you will eat your bread till you are fully fed. And you will dwell in your land securely. I will give you peace in the land. You will lie down and none will terrify. I will remove dangerous creatures from the land, and the sword will not destroy in your land. You will chase your enemies, and they will fall before you by the sword. Five of you will chase a hundred, and a hundred of you will chase ten thousand, and your enemies will fall before you by the sword. I will look favorably on you and will make you fruitful and multiply you, and I will establish my covenant with you. You will eat old grain long stored, and you will clear out old grain to make way for the new. I will put my dwelling in your midst, and I will not abhor you. I will stroll back and forth among you. I will be God for you, and you will be a people for me. I am Yahweh your God who brought you out of the land of Egypt, from being slaves. I broke the bars of your yoke, and I made you walk upright. (Lev. 26:1–13)

This passage makes various connections with the sabbath traditions in Genesis and Exodus. The opening and closing verses evoke the opening verses of the Decalogue or the Ten Commandments (Exod. 20:1–5; Deut. 5:6–9) and the sabbath law (Exod. 20:8–11; Deut. 5:12–15). The promise of timely rains and extraordinary agricultural yields recalls the lavish abundance of earth at creation. Genesis 1 envisions a world so exuberantly productive that its human governors will find their greatest challenge, not in coaxing fruit and grain from a reticent earth, but in managing the wild productivity of a world overflowing with life. Leviticus 26 also promises an idyllic world of flourishing life, where the annual cycles of planting and harvest begin to blur as Israel struggles to keep up with wildly productive earth. "Your threshing will overtake the vintage, the vintage will overtake the planting, and you will eat your bread till you are fully fed. You will dwell in your land securely" (cf. Amos 9:13). Grain will be stored for long periods of time and still be edible. New grain will fill the storage bins long before the old grain runs out. Food shortage will be a thing of the past. While Genesis 1:29–30 envisions a completely vegetarian world at creation, where no living creature must die for any other creature to live, Leviticus 26 foresees a land cleansed of dangerous creatures and violent enemies. It also borrows almost verbatim from Genesis 1. In the creation story, God blesses humans, male and female, and commands them to "be fruitful and multiply" (Gen. 1:28). In Leviticus 26:9, Yahweh promises to look after faithful Israel: "I will make you fruitful and multiply you. I will establish my covenant with you." In the ideology of ancient Near Eastern kingship, a fruitful and stable natural world is the result of a strong and upright rule. The idyllic world of Genesis 1 and Leviticus 26 is a sign of Yahweh's cosmic rule.

Finally, these verses envision the immediate relationship of God and people. God's dwelling will be found "in your midst." God will "stroll back and forth among you." Yahweh will be God for Israel, as Israel is a people for Yahweh. This intimacy will come because Yahweh "broke the bars of your yoke" and "caused you to walk upright" in freedom. Here the Priestly poet draws on a common ancient metaphor. The burden of debt and debt slavery is described as a "yoke" binding the debtor to the master who holds the claim. Freedom is described as "breaking the bar" of the yoke, "releasing" the straps, and letting the pack animal wiggle free (cf. the discussion of Neh. 5:13 in the previous chapter). The metaphor of breaking the yoke inhabits the same rhetorical universe as release (*shemittah*), the unbinding of burdens that drop off and allow the bearer to "walk upright," to "roll free" (*derôr*), unobstructed. The promise of jubilee is the promise of freedom and release.

Liberty to Captives, Good News to the Oppressed

> Arise! Shine! For your light has come! The glory of Yahweh has risen upon you! For darkness covers the earth and deep darkness the peoples. But upon you, Yahweh shines. God's glory appears over you! And nations will walk toward your light, and kings to the brightness of your dawn! (Isa. 60:1–3)

> I will set Peace as your overseer, and Righteousness as your taskmaster. No longer will "Violence!" be heard in your land, "Devastation!" or "Destruction!" within your borders. You will call your walls "Salvation!" and your gates "Praise!" The sun will no longer be your light by day, nor will the moon illuminate you for brightness. But Yahweh will be your light forever. Your God will be your glory. Your sun will no longer go down or your moon withdraw, for Yahweh will be your light forever. The days of your mourning will be completed. (Isa. 60:17–20)

> The spirit of my lord Yahweh is upon me, because Yahweh has anointed me, has sent me to bring good news to the oppressed, to bind up the brokenhearted, to proclaim liberty [*derôr*] to captives, to open the eyes of prisoners, to proclaim the year of Yahweh's favor and the day of our God's vengeance, to comfort all who mourn—to establish for the mourners of Zion, to give them a bridegroom's turban instead of ashes, the oil of celebration instead of mourning, the cloak of praise instead of a lifeless spirit… And they will build ancient ruins. Former devastations they will raise up, and they will repair ruined cities, the devastations of generations and generations… And you will be called priests of Yahweh. You will be said to be ministers of our God. (Isa. 61:1–6)

These verses were written at the end of Babylonian exile by an anonymous prophet, "Third Isaiah," who announces the return of deportees to Judah to rebuild Jerusalem. The poet heralds return as a proclamation of liberty (*derôr*) and describes the hoped-for restoration in exalted terms reminiscent of the idyllic world of Genesis 1 and Leviticus 26.

The symbolism of the shining light that announces this new era of liberty is well rooted in Mesopotamian practice. Announcements of liberty typically were signaled by raising a "golden torch" at the entrance gate of the released city or on the highway into the released region. The torch announced that this was a duty-free zone, a city or region exempted from taxes, forced labor, and military draft, cleared from debt and released from debt slavery. Moshe Weinfeld has collected several examples of torch-raising to signify royal release.[10] A Babylonian prophecy speaks of "a message by fire" that announces an establishment of *misharum* in the land. A letter to Ashurbanipal speaks of a "fire signal" that announces a release of prisoners.[11] A document regarding the claim of a field in the neo-Assyrian period opens with the following statement: "When my master (the king) lifted the golden torch for the city of Sippar and established *misharum* for the god Shamash who loves him…"[12] Shamash was the sun god, usually associated with justice and the administration of justice by kings in the ancient Near East.[13] It is not surprising, then, that the burning torch signified release, a radical act of royal justice.

Liberty is announced in Isaiah 60 by the lighting of a torch: "Arise! Shine! For your light has come! The glory of Yahweh has risen upon you!" Restored Israel is like the fortunate region illuminated by the golden torch of liberty at the start of a new king's reign. Restored and illuminated, Israel is a duty-free zone, a place of royal release from the burdens of debt, slavery, taxes, military impressment, and forced labor. Nations are drawn to the light of Israel's liberty, proclaimed forever by Yahweh. Though prompted by the royal decree of Cyrus, a human king, earlier proclaimed Israel's "messiah" by this prophet's literary precursor (Isa. 45:1), the liberty that Third Isaiah foresees for Israel announces the enthronement of a divine king. In a striking rhetorical twist, the prophet now assumes the role of messiah, the "anointed one" covered by the spirit of the royal lord Yahweh (61:1). The prophet is anointed to proclaim the good news that Yahweh's

---

[10]Weinfeld, *Social Justice*, 73, 91, 157.
[11]Ibid., 73.
[12]Ibid., 91, n. 70; 157, n. 20.
[13]Ibid., 51–54.

cosmic dominion is now established forever. The return of exiled Israel and the restoration of ruined Zion is the signal, the golden torch
that announces the universal liberty that celebrates the inauguration
of Yahweh's cosmic rule: "Nations will walk toward your light, and
kings to the brightness of your dawn!"

It is difficult to know whether the idyllic world envisioned in
these verses is eschatology or poetic hyperbole, whether, in these lofty
words, a prophet dreams of the distant future when God rules perfectly in the world, or a poet sees in the sudden reversal of exiled
Israel's fortune a ray of hope for a better life. Either way, the liberty
proclaimed and the torch raised announce the universal rule of Israel's
God. When God rules, the oppressed hear good news, the brokenhearted are bound up with loving care, captives are set free, and prisoners emerge from dark dungeons and open their eyes to the glorious
light of day. Liberty, justice, peace, freedom from violence—these are
signs of God's universal reign, announced by the raised torch of
freedom.

Finally, the golden torch of liberty lies in the historical background
of Jewish and Christian celebrations of Hanukkah and Advent. The
lighted candles of the Hanukkah menorah symbolize the purification
of the Jerusalem temple when the Maccabees liberated Judea from
foreign imperial rule. They also signal hope for universal reconcilia-
tion in the age of the Messiah. The lighted candles of Advent anticipate the "end times," the ultimate purpose and fulfillment of history,
the perfect and unmediated rule of God in the world. In both celebrations, the candle flame—like the golden torch in ancient proclamations of liberty—signals the beginning of a new dominion, the
reign of God in the world.

Summary

Sabbath-year and jubilee traditions are utopian in many respects.
It is difficult to understand exactly what the proponents of these laws
had in mind and how the laws could be enacted. A total ban on agriculture in sabbath year and jubilee, for example, would lead to mass
starvation. Universal seventh- (and fiftieth-) year fallowing "is not
sensible farming," since the soil needs to lie fallow more frequently
for proper replenishment. But agricultural sabbath-year and jubilee
laws do not have a practical intent. These laws establish the theological principle that God "owns" the land and frees it from bondage to

any human lord—just as God "bought" Israel from slavery. Israel must respect the integrity of the land apart from its usefulness, even as the historic enemies of Israel learned to respect the integrity of Israel, redeemed and freed by Yahweh.

Passages in Nehemiah 10 and 1 Maccabees 6 that might be read as sabbath-year agricultural bans more likely refer to debt and rent relief along the lines of Deuteronomy 15 and Exodus 23.

Rabbis late in the second temple period thought that sabbath-year and jubilee laws no longer carried the force of biblical authority because jubilee had to be observed by "all of Israel" "in the land." The reality of diaspora meant that proper observance of jubilee (and sabbath year) was not possible. Elements of sabbath year, such as debt release, were enforced by rabbinical authority as a moral lesson so that Israel would not forget the jubilee mandated by Torah, but were moot under current circumstances.

Jubilee laws are a diverse collection that are mostly impractical as social policy. But they establish important and revolutionary theological and ethical principles. Jubilee laws on slavery and land redistribution offer systemic solutions to systemic social problems of ancient monarchy.

Jubilee is connected rhetorically with the sacred narratives of Israel. Announcing it on the Day of Atonement associates jubilee with purification for an encounter with God. The trumpet blast that announces jubilee recalls the theophany at Mount Sinai, where Israel met Yahweh for the first time and received the words of the Torah. In that narrative account (Exod. 19—20), trumpet blasts signal the start of direct conversation between Moses and Yahweh. Jubilee observance is a Sinai experience for Israel, an encounter with God.

The anonymous postexilic prophet who wrote Isaiah 60—61 draws from the store of symbols associated with royal proclamations of liberty in the ancient world to signal the advent of a new dominion—the universal reign of Yahweh on earth. The symbolism of the golden torch lifted to signal a royal proclamation of liberty undergirds the prophet's exhortation to "rise! shine! for your light has come!" It also lies in the symbolic background when Jews and Christians light the candles of Hanukkah and Advent. They burn as signs of purification, preparation, and hope for the universal reign of God.

Finally, jubilee and sabbath-year traditions have multiple connections with the sabbath-day stories in Genesis and Exodus.

6

SABBATH AND CREATION

The two foundational sabbath narratives in the Bible associate sabbath with creation. In the first story, sabbath is portrayed as a fundamental principle of the universe, the climax of the world's creation at the beginning of time. In the second story, sabbath is the culmination of Israel's national story of creation: the exodus from Egypt and victory at the sea. These two narratives literarily precede all other biblical references to sabbath and together form the canonical lens through which all biblical sabbath, sabbath-year, and jubilee passages are read. Both stories offer a utopian vision of the world that stands in sharp contrast to the social-economic reality experienced by agrarian households under ancient monarchy. They function as prophetic critique of the status quo and visionary hope for a better world.

Sabbath: Creation's Delight

When God began creating the sky and earth, the world was shapeless chaos. Darkness was blanketing the deep, while an awesome wind was sweeping across the surface of the waters. God said, "Let there be light!" There was light. God saw the light as delightful!

79

Then God made a division between the light and the darkness. God called the light "day," and called the darkness "night." So there was evening and morning, day one.

Then God said, "Let there be a hammered-out surface in the waters to separate water from water!" So God made the hammered-out surface to separate the water below the hammered-out surface from the water above the hammered-out surface. And it happened just that way. And God called the hammered-out surface, "sky." So there was evening and morning, day two.

Then God said, "Let the water below the sky be collected into a single place so the dry land can appear!" And it happened just that way. God called the dry land "earth" and called the collected water "seas." God saw this as delightful!

Then God said, "Let the earth sprout sprouts, seed-bearing plants, fruit trees that make all kinds of fruit with seed in them, all over the earth!" And it happened just that way. The earth produced sprouting plants, seed-bearing seed of all kinds, as well as all kinds of fruit-producing, seed-bearing trees. And God saw this as delightful! So there was evening and morning, day three.

Then God said, "Let there be lights in the hammered-out surface of the sky to separate the day from the night! Let them serve as omens and markers of seasons, of days and years. Let them radiate light in the hammered-out surface of the sky, illuminating the earth." And it happened just that way. God made two great lights—the big light to govern the day, the small light to govern the night—and the stars. God inset them in the hammered-out surface of the sky to illuminate the earth, to govern daytime and night, and to separate the light from the darkness. And God saw this as delightful! So there was evening and morning, day four.

Then God said, "Let the waters swarm with a swarm of living creatures, while the bird flies over the earth, across the hammered-out surface of the sky!" So God created the great sea monsters and every creeping living thing that swarms the water—all kinds of them—as well as all kinds of winged bird. And God saw this as delightful! Then God blessed them, saying, "Be fruitful! Become numerous! Fill the waters of the seas, while the bird becomes numerous on the earth." So there was evening and morning, day five.

Then God said, "Let the land produce all kinds of living creatures—beast and creepy thing, all kinds of land creatures." And it happened just that way. God made all kinds of land creatures—all kinds of beast and all kinds of things that creep on the ground. And God saw this as delightful!

Then God said, "Let's make a human in our own image, according to our likeness, so they can rule the fish of the sea and the bird of the sky and the beast and all the land, as well as all the creeping things that creep on the land." So God created the human, created it in the image, the very image of God!—created them male and female. Then God blessed them, and God told them, "Be fruitful! Become numerous! Fill the earth and master it. Rule the fish of the sea, the bird of the sky and every living thing that creeps on the land." Then God said, "Look, I am giving you every plant with seed-bearing seed on the surface of the whole earth, and every tree with seed-bearing tree fruit in it. These will serve as food for you and for every land creature and for every bird of the sky and for everything that creeps on the land that has the breath of life in it—every green plant as food!" And it happened just that way!

God looked at everything made. It was especially delightful! So there was evening and morning, day six.

So the sky and the earth and all their host were finished. So God finished, on the seventh day, all the work God had done. God rested, on the seventh day, from all the work God had done. And God blessed the seventh day and sanctified it, because, on it, God rested from all the work God had created to do.

These are the generations of the sky and the earth when they were created. (Gen. 1:1—2:4a)

The account of creation that opens Genesis invites the reader to view subsequent biblical stories with eyes of sabbath joy and praise. Though historically the latter of two creation stories at the beginning of Genesis (ca. late 500s B.C.E.), the seven-day creation narrative introduces the book and serves as the introduction to the Bible as a whole. Universal blessing and sabbath joy, the thematic substance of this creation story, form the lens through which Israel's subsequent sacred history comes into focus.

Themes of natural abundance and personal self-restraint stand at the heart of the story. It portrays a created world fundamentally benevolent and able to produce enough to sustain prosperous human life. This theme of natural abundance is coupled, however, with a theme of self-restraint. By God's own precedent, rest is woven into the fabric of the universe. Periodic self-limitation, deliberate relinquishment of power to work the world and control it, is by sabbath example a cosmic principle. Creation climaxes and finally coheres in sabbath rest. It is the glue that holds the world together.

Stirring the Cosmic Soup

This story portrays creation as a progressive movement from chaos to order. "When God began to create the sky and the earth," the story begins, "the world was shapeless chaos."

The syntax of the first two verses is awkward and difficult to translate. The traditional translation leaves a confusing picture. "In the beginning, God created the heavens and the earth. The earth was without form and void..." (RSV). A logical problem is introduced with the rhyming word pair *tohû wabohû*, translated by RSV as "without form and void."

Tohû appears by itself several times in the Hebrew Scriptures.[1] Though its precise meaning varies, *tohû* in every case signifies something empty and wild, without shape or coherence. Often it describes uncultivated wilderness and stands in contrast with the ecological and social order of land successfully claimed by agriculture. *Tohû* is "unstructured" and "useless" land, full of undomesticated and dangerous beasts that devour crops, raid flocks, and attack humans who wander there. *Tohû* is anti-agriculture, and, therefore, hostile to human life.

In three cases, *tohû* is paired with *bohû* (Isa. 34:11; Jer. 4:23; Gen. 1:2). *Bohû*, which never appears in the Bible without *tohû*, is

---

[1]Deut. 32:10; 1 Sam. 12:21; Isa. 24:10; 29:21; 40:17, 23; 41:29; 44:9; 45:18, 19; 49:4; 59:4; Job 6:18; 12:24; 26:7; Ps. 107:40.

probably a nonsense word made to sound like *tohû* and meant to communicate more of the same, along the lines of "itsy bitsy" and "teeny weeny." If *tohû* is that which is empty, uncultivated, disordered, dangerous, and useless, then *tohû wabohû* is doubly so.

Tohû wabohû is the uncontrollable chaos that threatens the social and ecological order imposed on the world by agriculture: by planted crops, by grazing flocks and by herds, by farms, homes, villages, and cities. It is unpredictable and unmanageable disaster that breaks without warning and threatens to destroy settled life—agrarian society's worst nightmare. According to Genesis 1, it is what the universe was when God began creating. It is also what the universe would return to without God's constant power and care. Creation is the imposition of agrarian order on primordial wilderness. The disorder that remains will be pushed to the margins of the zone of life, where it is contained for now, but always threatens to violate the boundaries set by God at creation.

The traditional translation of the first two sentences of Genesis creates logical and chronological problems. "In the beginning, God created the heavens and the earth; and the earth was without form and void [*tohû wabohû*]." The reader is placed in a logical conundrum by this translation's suggestion that the first thing God created was an earth that had no form or substance. To "create" an "uncreated" earth is nonsense. The traditional translation also presents a chronological problem further down in the story (vv. 6–10) where sky and earth are said to be created for the first time on days two and three, respectively. How could this be, if God had already created them "in the beginning," on day one?

These problems of logic and chronology can be solved in one of two ways. Many scholars keep the traditional translation but take verse 1 as an introductory overview of the entire creation story to follow. It is, in effect, the story's title: "In the Beginning God Created the Sky and the Earth." Verse 2 begins the narrative proper: "Now the earth was shapeless chaos." It is equally plausible, however, to read verse 1 as a subordinate, temporal clause that modifies the main clause in verse 2: "When God began creating the sky and the earth, the world was shapeless chaos."

In either case, the story begins with *tohû wabohû*, the primordial chaos that existed when God started to speak an ordered world into being. The first two verses set the stage for God's activity, which begins in verse 3 with God's command, "Let there be light." At the dawn of creation, the world was shapeless chaos, useless wilderness, dark, deep, and fiercely windy water.

The narrative here adopts the common ancient Near Eastern view that the world is shaped by divine will out of a watery abyss (cf. Pss. 24:2; 104:5–9). This creative act typically is portrayed as a battle against primeval sea monsters or the sea itself, personified as a god (Pss. 74:13–15; Isa. 51:9; Job 3:8; 38:8–11).[2] Creation is a process of separating and measuring, setting boundaries, bringing form and shape to that which is formless and wild. Created things have substance and form. They can be visualized. Like plowed and planted, watered and tended rows of crops at the edge of desert wilderness, created things can be distinguished, their shapes made out among the meaningless confusion of disordered chaos.

God begins creating by shedding light on dark chaos and setting a boundary between darkness and light to distinguish day and night. Visibility comes to dark, shapeless chaos. The universe is introduced to the most fundamental instrument of measure and order in an agrarian world: time.

Then God separates the waters of chaos by putting a solid surface in their midst. The surface, *raqîa'*, was solid and malleable like metal, as we see in verses 14–17, and 20b, where the heavenly bodies are inset in the sky like jewels in a bracelet (cf. Job 37:18). This onomatopoeic Hebrew word mimics the sound of hammering metal. In verbal form, it is what a smith does, hammering out a copper bowl or silver plate (cf. Exod. 39:3; Num. 17:3–4; Isa. 40:19; Jer. 10:9). In the common ancient Near Eastern view, the sky was thought to be a dome set in place by the gods to hold back the waters of chaos and create a zone of order where life is possible. The created world is a "biosphere," a "bubble of life" suspended in watery chaos, which is kept out from horizon to horizon by the circle of dry land and from above to below by the solid surface of the sky and the firm foundations of the earth. Biblical authors shared this ancient Near Eastern view. So the sky is portrayed as a solid dome (Ezek. 1:22–26; 10:1) or a canopy stretched out high over the earth (Isa. 40:22; 44:24; Prov. 8:27–28; Job 22:14; 37:18) to hold back the waters of chaos.

On the third day, God further separates the waters below, causing dry land to appear. The emergence of land allows vegetation to

---

[2]See the Babylonian and Ugaritic creation stories, *Enuma Elish* and *Baal and Yamm*.

grow. On days four through six, God insets heavenly bodies into the solid surface of the sky and summons into existence swarms of living creatures to swim the seas, to fly between earth and sky, and to crawl, walk, and feed on the land. Throughout, the creative process is a progressive ordering of watery chaos, an act of separation and collection that allows solid things to appear from the primordial abyss.

A "Fat" and Prosperous World

One of the key words this story uses to describe what God is doing is *bara'*, "create"—a word used interchangeably with *'asah*, "make." Elsewhere, human beings are said to "make" (*'asah*) things. But the Bible reserves *bara'* for God. Humans "make," and so does God. But God alone "creates."

A secondary meaning of *bara'* gives a more graphic picture of the process described by this verb. In the *hiphil* form of the verb in 1 Samuel 2:29, *bara'* means "to fatten oneself." As an adjective, *bara'* means "fat."[3] Outside the Hebrew Bible, *bara'* refers to separating fats from a liquid, skimming cream from milk. As its secondary meaning illustrates, *bara'* well describes God's creative activity in a story that portrays creation as the progressive separating and collecting of primordial waters to allow the solids to appear—sky, earth, and heavenly bodies. The created world is the cream that rises to the top of watery chaos, separated and collected by God.

Bara' is appropriate for another reason as well. In the biblical world, fatness connotes wealth, prosperity, and health (cf. Jacob's blessing in Gen. 27:28). This idea undergirds the symbolism of anointing, a ceremony associated with the monarchy. By anointing with "fatness"—usually olive oil—the participants ritually celebrated or petitioned God for abundance, fertility, safety, and wholeness.[4] This understanding explains the symbolic significance of anointing in connection with healing and restoration[5] and with the election of a king. Anointing symbolically expressed the hope and expectation that the

---

[3]Gen. 41:2, 4, 5, 7, 18, 20; Judg. 3:17; 1 Kgs. 5:3; Ps. 73:4; Ezek. 34:3, 20; Hab. 1:16; Zech. 11:6; Dan. 1:15.

[4]Cf. Jacob's "anointing" the pillar at Bethel, Gen. 28:18–22; 31:13; 35:1–15; the "anointment" of tabernacle and priesthood, Exod. 30:22–38; Leviticus 7:36; 8:10–13; Num. 7:1; and metaphorically, "the oil of gladness" in Ps. 45:7 and Heb. 1:9.

[5]2 Sam. 12:20; Isa. 61:1//Luke 4:18; Ezek. 16:9; Dan. 10:3; 2 Chr. 28:15; Mark 6:13; Acts 10:38; related to burial in Mark 14:8; 16:1; Luke 7:46; and John 12:3.

new reign would bring prosperity, fertility, stability, and peace to the nation.[6] The "anointed one" could expect military success and prosperity[7] and had grounds for complaint if such good fortune was not forthcoming (Ps. 89:20–51). This expectation explains David's reluctance to harm Yahweh's anointed king, Saul (1 Sam. 24:6; 2 Sam. 1:14, 16), and the deep sense of crisis felt at the death of a king. David's curse of Mount Gilboa, the place where Saul and Jonathan fell in battle, is particularly poignant in this regard: "You mountains of Gilboa, let there be no dew or rain upon you, nor bounteous fields! For there the shield of the mighty was defiled, the shield of Saul, anointed with oil no more" (2 Sam. 1:21, NRSV).

The stability, security, and natural abundance associated with monarchy and expressed in the ceremony of anointing is claimed for all creation in Genesis 1 by the use of *bara'* to describe how God brings the world into being. *Bara'*—the word that describes the seven "fat" cows in Pharaoh's famous dream (Gen. 41:2–20), the rich and lavish food of Israel's enemy (Hab. 1:16), and the miraculous physical health of Daniel's kosher vegetarians (Dan. 1:15)—sets up a double entendre in the Genesis 1 creation story. God "creates" a "fat" world, a rich and lavish overflow of goodness, abundant and life-giving at its very core. In this creation story, universal prosperity is simply the way of the world as God called it into being and intends it to be.

A World of Delight

The double nuance of *bara'*—"to create" and "to be fat"—is reinforced in the narrative by God's appraisal of the creative work in progress. The declaration, "God saw that it was good (*tôb*)," runs like a litany through the story. But the full meaning of *tôb* is not captured by the English word, "good." *Tôb* may also imply joy and delight, and I think it does so in this story. In this reading of the narrative, *tôb* is by no means a neutral appraisal of God's creative work in progress. To the contrary, the *tôb* refrain expresses God's intense pleasure at creation's every detail. It is God's cosmic "Wow!" as each major phase of creation unfolds. To express the passion that I think is implicit in God's appraisal of the "fat" world of God's creation, I translate *tôb*

---

[6]1 Sam. 2:10; 9:16; 10:1; 16:1, 6, 13; 2 Sam. 2:4; 5:3//1 Chr. 11:3; 2 Sam. 22:51; 23:1; 1 Kgs. 1:39, 45//1 Chr. 29:22; 2 Kgs. 11:12//2 Chr. 23:11; 2 Kings 23:30. See the discussion, "the ideology of kingship" in chapter 1 above.

[7]1 Sam. 12:7; Pss. 2:2; 18:50; 20:6; 28:8; 84:9; 132:17; Isa. 45:1 Hab. 3:13.

with the English word "delightful," yielding the refrain "God saw this as delightful!"

Significantly in Genesis 1, the delightfulness of the universe does not depend on human judgment. God values creation as delightful from the very first appearance of light, long before human beings enter the picture. It is true that God first declares the universe *tôb me'od*, "especially delightful," only after human beings are created (1:31). But it is "everything God made," not humanity alone, that is so valued. Unrestrained joy, wild delight is a characteristic of creation long before humans are made. The universe is delightful, not because human beings declare it so, but because that is the way God made it.

Sabbath Rest, the Crown of Creation

According to the chapter division imposed on the biblical text a millennium and a half after the story was written, the end of day six (1:31) marks the end of a distinct narrative unit. The next sentence (2:1) begins a new chapter that includes the sabbath day and the first episode of the garden of Eden story.

Whatever the original intent of such a chapter division, its effect is to devalue sabbath and exalt humanity. It implies that the story ends after day six, with humans created male and female "in the image of God" and authorized to "rule the earth and master it." It emphasizes work over rest and encourages an anthropocentric reading of the world that has had destructive consequences in the modern age. It also runs counter to the narrative logic of the story.

Literary clues in the story itself suggest that the narrative unit properly ends at 2:4a. Hebrew writers used various techniques to mark the beginning and end of a narrative unit. Sometimes they structured the story on a formal pattern. This story, for example, is patterned on a seven-day week, suggesting that the story ends when the week ends, after day seven. Sometimes Hebrew writers mark a narrative unit by repeating in the last sentence key words from the first sentence. Genesis 2:4a repeats key words of 1:1: "When God began to create the sky and the earth" (1:1) and "these are the generations of the sky and the earth, when they were created" (2:4a). These verses act as literary bookends, setting the boundaries of the narrative unit. They and everything in between belong together.

Furthermore, 1:2—2:3 has a very carefully crafted literary structure. Days one to three parallel days four to six in symmetrical fashion.

Day 1	light day/night	**Day 4**	heavenly lights mark days, nights, seasons
Day 2	sky to separate waters above/below	**Day 5**	sky animals, water animals
Day 3	dry land arises	**Day 6**	land animals/humans

This symmetry helps the narrative cohere as a unit but also highlights the verses of the story (1:1–2 and 2:1–4a) that fall outside the pattern.

The verses at the story's beginning and end form an antithetical parallel. The end reverses the beginning. The introduction (1:1–2) portrays the universe as shapeless watery chaos when God began creating. Deep darkness engulfed everything that existed, making it impossible to distinguish matter, space, or time. The world was so fractured and fragmented, so atomized, that nothing could be made out among the undifferentiated chaos, the indistinguishable nothingness (*tohû wabohû*) of the primordial universe.

The concluding verses of the story portray an exact reversal. The description of the seventh day begins by asserting the world's wholeness, its distinctive somethingness. The sentence structure of 2:1–2a drives home the sense of completeness and wholeness by repeating in verbal and nominal form a word that means "whole, complete, full, total": "And they were finished [*calah*], sky and earth and all [*cal*] their host, and he finished [*calah*] the work he did." The sky and earth began as shapeless nothing, but now have become a completed universe. The clause that follows (2:2b) expands the theme of completion with the verb *shabat*, "to rest, cease, stop." This is the verbal form of the noun *shabbat* that comes into English as "sabbath": "and God stopped/rested on the seventh day from all the work he did." In 1:1–2, God begins creative work on the formless abyss. In 2:1–4a, God completes work on a world that now has shape and substance.

God's ability to rest is also a sign of God's sovereign rule in creation. Elsewhere in the Bible, "rest"[8] describes political stability, the ability of a people or a monarch to secure order and successfully govern the land. Yahweh grants Israel rest from all its enemies at the time

---

[8]These references have a different verbal root, *nwh*, but the idea is the same.

of the conquest (Deut. 3:20; Josh. 1:13–15; 23:1). Yahweh does the same for David (2 Sam. 7:1, 11; contra 1 Kgs. 5:3) and Solomon (1 Kgs. 5:4; 8:56; 1 Chr. 22:9). In the latter passages, rest is associated with dynastic election and the building of Yahweh's temple in Jerusalem. David and Solomon are able to consider building Yahweh's house because Yahweh has granted them rest from their enemies round about. Rest is security, political stability, a firm and benevolent grip on power to preserve life-giving order. Rest is *shalom*. God rests at the end of creation because God is able to rest. God's benevolent rule in the universe is unchallenged. Sabbath rest is a celebration of God's enthronement as universal sovereign.

A Blessing in Time

In the narrative logic of the story, time is the fundamental instrument of cosmic order. The creation and blessing of time brackets the creation of the universe. God first creates light and distinguishes day and night, setting into motion the universal regulator by which all the internal clocks of life are set. The daily movement of the sun sets the biological, agricultural, and social rhythms of earth. Unshaped chaos is timeless, without day and night to regulate life. Time is the necessary first step toward order, the foundation of life. God creates universal time on day one and sacred time on day seven. The consecration of a sacred day, a sabbath, signals the completion of the world, God's final ordering of a life-supporting universe out of timeless chaos. Time, the most basic instrument of order in creation, is now itself ordered. Sabbath is the final piece of the creative process by which the world comes into being. It is the crowning touch, the cosmic sign that God's universal and benevolent dominion is fully extended and secure. Sabbath completes the life-giving universe and provides its ultimate coherence.

The seventh day differs from other days of creation in form as well as content. Each of the previous six days is introduced with the formula "then God said" (vv. 3, 6, 9, 14, 20, 24) and ends with the formula "there was evening and morning, day one," and so on (vv. 5, 8, 13, 19, 23, 31).

The seventh-day narrative breaks the pattern. It opens with an action, not a word: "God finished" rather than "God said." It also identifies the day in the *opening* clause, not at the end: "God finished, on the seventh day..." (2:2a). "Seventh day" is repeated three times (2:2a, 2b, 3a), as opposed to the single identification at the end of each of the previous six days. The seventh-day account does not end with the expected formula, "there was evening and morning." Breaking the pattern in this way emphasizes the uniqueness of the seventh day and opens the door to an eschatological interpretation. Literarily, the sun has not yet set on God's sabbath.

The extraordinary character of the seventh day has a theological foundation, clarified in verse 3: "God blessed the seventh day and made it holy, because on it God rested from all the work God created to do." This is the only day God "blesses." Otherwise in this story, only sea creatures, birds (1:22), and human beings created in the image of God (1:28) are "blessed." In these cases, God's blessing is coupled with the admonition to "be fertile and numerous," a connection reiterated in the covenant blessing of Israel's ancestors (Gen. 12:2; 17:20; 22:17; 26:3–4, 24). Blessing is fundamentally about fertility, long-term prosperity, and flourishing life. In Genesis, blessing expresses a double responsibility. God's promise calls for the world's response. God's blessing is also God's command. To be blessed is to flourish, and to flourish is to respond appropriately to God's command. Blessing carries the responsibility to live a blessed life.

Blessing is fundamentally relational, an expression of goodwill for the prosperity of another. At its most literal level, the Hebrew root, *barak* ("bless"), describes "bending the knee," an act of humility associated with worship and praise. Secondarily, it refers to greeting or well-wishing. In the Hebrew Scriptures, God blesses humans, and humans are called upon to bless God and one another. In all these cases, respect for the intrinsic value and welfare of the other undergirds the act of blessing. When God blesses humans, God declares us worthy and expresses desire for our well-being. When humans bless God, we declare God worthy and express gratitude for God's goodwill toward us.

Sabbath, as blessed time, is the cosmic pole around which all other time coheres. Sabbath establishes all of life as a celebration of the worthiness of God and God's created world. Sabbath is a sign of God's benevolent desire for the world. By observing the blessed sabbath, the world expresses gratitude to the God who calls us into flourishing life.

In the Image of God

In this story, God blesses human beings (1:28) immediately after creating them male and female, "in the image of God" (1:26–27). It is appropriate that blessing is connected with gender difference in this narrative, since blessing in Genesis usually has to do with offspring. Sexual differentiation, "male and female," is explicitly mentioned in the story only in reference to human beings, though other living beings are also sexually differentiated. The storyteller is making more than simply a biological point here. By highlighting the maleness and femaleness of humans, the narrative stresses the complementary diversity of persons who are at once the same (human) and different (male and female). Humans are related, not identical. We are interpersonal at our very core. We are social beings. Our humanity springs from mutually supportive relationships between diverse people. The unity and survival of the species reside in its complementary diversity, a biological fact of all sexually reproducing species, but a social-psychological reality of human existence that Genesis 1 finds worth emphasizing.

Appropriately, the image of God in which humans, male and female, are created is plural: "Let's make a human in *our* own image, with *our* own likeness" (v. 26). The plurals here reflect a view of divine authority that mirrors the household and royal court. God works by decree. In a well-functioning ancient Near Eastern monarchy, the king's word was law.[9] Every enactment of a royal decree was proof of the king's sovereign power. In Genesis 1, the refrain, "Let there be... and there was," indicates that God's royal grip on power in the universe is secure. God's cosmic throne rises in the narrative shadows of every utterance. But now, in the creation of women and men, the stage lights are turned up and the divine court is explicitly revealed: "Let us create a human in our own image, so that they might rule the earth!"

The unique role of human beings in the world is suggested by the syntax of the compound sentence in verse 26, a structure that

---

[9]This understanding of the power of the royal word is what moves the plot, precipitating and ultimately resolving the crises in Daniel 6 (see especially vv. 8, 24–27) and Esther 1:19–20; 8:8.

suggests purpose or result.[10] "Let us make a human in our image, in our own likeness, *so that* they might rule the earth." While there is room for theological debate about the precise nature of the image of God, there is no question about its purpose in this passage. Humans are created male and female in the image of God so they can rule. The authority and power to govern is what makes humans "like God." Created in the image of God, every human being is royal.

While the monarchist metaphor hardly fits today's more egalitarian and democratic theologies, the notion of divine and human sovereignty reflected in the passage provides a helpful corrective to the more destructive forms of individualist ideology pervasive in American culture. As we saw earlier, sovereignty in the ancient world was rooted in a strong sense of responsibility to the collective welfare of the nation. The king was the householder of the nation—the "father and mother," the "shepherd" of the people. Kings may have been despots, but at least ideally they operated out of concern for the well-being of the whole. Kings' honor depended on their protecting and caring for the weak.

God's attentive care and generosity toward the world in the creation story is a function of God's sovereignty, a matter of honor. So too, humans, by virtue of their creation in the image of God to rule and master the earth, have a special responsibility for the welfare of all living creatures, especially the most vulnerable. By portraying God's sovereign rule as fundamentally benevolent, Genesis 1 authorizes God-resembling humans to exercise power in the world with responsibility and generosity.

The Image of God as Community Blessing

A common thread of blessing ties together living creatures (1:22), humans (1:28), and the seventh day (2:3). The connection of blessing with fertility and, therefore, survival and prosperity makes the use of blessing language perfectly intelligible in the case of animals and humans. It is not at all clear, however, what it means to "bless" a day.

---

[10]A cohortative clause ("let us…"), followed immediately by a clause that begins with a non-converted imperfect verb ("and they will…"), normally expresses purpose or result. Ronald J. Williams, *Hebrew Syntax: An Outline*, 2d ed. (Toronto: University of Toronto Press, 1976), paragraph 187, 35. Thomas O. Lambdin, *Introduction to Biblical Hebrew* (New York: Charles Scribner's Sons, 1971), 119.

The narrative structure of 2:3, at first glance, does little to clarify what it means to "bless" the seventh day. Here the verb "to bless" is paired with a word (*qiddash*) usually translated "to hallow, consecrate, or keep holy." The basic meaning is "to set apart." Holiness has to do with things set apart from normal use or activity.

Things set apart were "clean," a quality that biblical texts describe in almost physical terms. Many of the normal things of the everyday world were "impure, unclean," but holy things were "pure, clean." The distinction expressed a material rather than a moral reality. The mundane world was neither shameful nor wicked in itself. "Impure" things were not evil. They were dirty. Dirty hands are not "sinful," but they should be washed before they handle food.

Holiness or purity rules told Israel how it should handle things specially associated with God. Holy things should be removed from everyday use to keep them clean. They should be handled with utmost care under scrupulously observed procedures performed by persons properly cleansed from the contaminants of everyday life. The creation story tells us that the seventh day is "made holy," set apart from the everyday, and thus invested with purity.

Given the close connection in this story between blessing and progeny, it is a little surprising to read that the seventh day is both "blessed" and "made holy." In the Priestly code, procreative acts make people ritually impure for a while (Lev. 15:18; cf. Exod. 19:15; 1 Sam. 21:4–6), and childbirth (Lev. 12:2–5) makes the mother unclean for forty or eighty days, depending on the sex of the child.

Genesis leaves no ambiguity, however, about the reason the seventh day is blessed and set apart. God "made it holy because on it God rested from all the work God created to do" (2:3b). Even as blessing and holiness are held in subtle tension, so too are God's rest and God's work. In a delightful twist, "rest" is a verb in this passage and "work" is a noun. Sabbath rest is active, not passive. Furthermore, it has meaning only in reference to God's creative work. Sabbath rest is not the absence of work. It is work's fulfillment. It celebrates creative labor. Rather than saying "no" to work, sabbath says "enough for now."

Working people might be expected to welcome a mandated day of rest. The self-restraint of sabbath observance, however, requires a leap of faith, a firm confidence that the world will continue to operate benevolently for a day without human labor, that God is willing and able to provide enough for good life. Sabbath promises seven days of prosperity for six days of work. It operates on the assumption that human life and prosperity exceed human productivity. We get more out of life than we put into it.

This is the key to understanding how sabbath brings together blessing and holiness. Holiness is the outcome of creation's God-given wholeness. Abundance is the wellspring of its purity. Life is more than human effort, and the surplus is witness to the transcendent and benevolent power of God. On the seventh day, at the completion of God's creative work, life in its fullness is declared holy, because life and everything that sustains it is the blessed gift of God. The abundance that makes sabbath rest possible amply proves God's providential care. In the sabbath celebration of abundant life, holiness and blessing converge, the sacred world and the profane embrace.

No Shortage, No Excess: Sabbath Manna for a Wilderness People

The whole congregation of the Israelites grumbled against Moses and Aaron in the wilderness. The Israelites said to them, "If only we had died at the hand of Yahweh in the land of Egypt when we were sitting at pots of meat and eating bread till we were full. You have surely brought us out to this wilderness to kill this whole assembly with famine!" Then Yahweh said to Moses, "Look! I am causing bread to rain from heaven for you! The people will go out and gather a day's worth each day, because I am testing whether they will follow my instruction or not. On the sixth day, they will prepare what they have brought in, and it will be twice as much as they gather every other day." So Moses and Aaron said to all the Israelites, "In the evening, you will know that Yahweh brought you out of the land of Egypt. And in the morning, you will see the glory of Yahweh who has heard your grumbling…

Now when Aaron spoke to all the congregation of Israelites, they faced the wilderness and suddenly the glory of Yahweh appeared in the cloud. Yahweh said to Moses, "I have heard the grumbling of the Israelites. Say the following to them: At twilight you will eat meat and in the morning you will fill up on bread, because I am Yahweh your God!"

In the evening, quails came up and covered the camp. In the morning, there was a layer of dew all around the camp. When the layer of dew lifted, there on the surface of the wilderness was a thin flaky substance, as thin as frost on the ground.

When the Israelites saw this, they said to each other, "What's that?"[11]—because they did not know what it was. Moses said to them, "That is the bread that Yahweh has given you to eat! This is what Yahweh has commanded: Gather as much of it as each needs to eat, an omer per person, according to the number of your people, everyone gathering for the people in their own tents.

So the Israelites did it just that way. Some gathered more, and some gathered less. But when they measured with an omer, the ones with more had no surplus and the ones with less had no shortage. They all gathered exactly what they needed to eat. Then Moses said to them, "No one should keep leftovers till morning." But they did not listen to Moses. People kept some leftovers till morning. It bred worms and spoiled. And Moses was furious with them.

Every morning they gathered it, each according to his need. When the sun grew hot, it melted. But on the sixth day, they gathered a double portion of bread, two omers for each one. And all the leaders of the congregation came to tell Moses.

He told them, "This is what Yahweh has said. Tomorrow is a complete rest (*shabbatôn*), a holy sabbath (*shabbat qodesh*) for Yahweh. Bake whatever you bake, and boil whatever you boil. Set aside any leftovers you have to be kept until morning. So they set it aside until morning just like Moses had commanded. And it did not spoil, and there were no worms in it. Moses said, "Eat it today, because today is sabbath for Yahweh. Today you will not find it in the field.

---

[11]This is an ancient version of Abbott and Costello's "Who's on first?" routine. The Hebrew is *man hû'*—something like, "what the heck is that?"—a pun on *man*, "manna." The people don't know it, but the answer is embedded in their question: "What's that?" (*man hû'*). "That's manna!" (*hû man*).

You will gather it for six days, but on the seventh day, sabbath, it will not be there."

So on the seventh day, some of the people went out to gather, and they found nothing. And Yahweh said to Moses, "How long are you people going to refuse to keep my commands and my instructions? Look, Yahweh has given you the sabbath. That's why he is giving you two day's worth of bread on the sixth day. Each of you stay put! No one go out of your place on the seventh day!"

So the Israelites named it "Manna."

… Moses said, "This is the thing Yahweh commanded: A full omer of it must be kept for your future generations, so they can see the bread that I fed you in the wilderness when I brought you out of the land of Egypt." Moses said to Aaron, "Take one jar and put a full omer of manna there. Place it before Yahweh to be kept for your future generations." (Exod. 16:2–33)

God's providential care also provides the major theme of the sabbath-manna story in Exodus 16.

Obvious tensions within the text indicate a complex history of development, the threads of which are not easily disentangled. The chapter incorporates material from the two major preexilic literary sources, J and E, and has undergone a substantial revision at the hands of a Priestly editor. There is a very different parallel story in Numbers 11 that highlights the "gift" of quail and says little about manna. The Exodus story reverses that emphasis and explicitly ties the gift of manna to the origin of sabbath.

In its present placement in the book of Exodus, the sabbath-manna story immediately follows the celebration of Israel's victory at the Sea of Reeds, one of the central stories of biblical faith, and, in many important respects, a story of Israel's origin as a people. Not surprisingly then, the long hymn of chapter 15 describes Israel's final escape from Pharaoh with rhetoric deeply rooted in the creation traditions of the ancient Near East. The Priestly creation-sabbath story in Genesis 1 portrays sabbath as the culmination of the natural world's creation by God. Exodus 16 places the origin of sabbath immediately after the creation of Israel as a free people redeemed by Yahweh. Both "creation" stories lead to sabbath. It is important to understand the mythic background of the rhetoric in Exodus 15 to see the creation motifs and to grasp their significance for the interpretation of the sabbath-manna story in Exodus 16.

For many ancient Near Eastern cultures, the sea was associated with the watery chaos out of which the ordered universe was created. In Mesopotamian and Canaanite creation myths, the sea was a raging goddess or god who had to be conquered by a divine hero—usually the god of rainstorms and crop fertility. In the Babylonian creation story, *Enuma Elish*, the primordial sea goddess Tiamat rages and threatens to destroy order in the universe. The gods cower. Only the storm god Marduk will confront Tiamat and the serpentine sea monsters who fight on her behalf. After a long and fierce battle, Marduk manages to blow a great wind down Tiamat's open mouth and then strikes her with an arrow. She explodes. Chaos is defeated, and an orderly, habitable world can now be formed. In ancient Canaanite culture, the storm god's name was Baal, and the sea god's name was Yamm, but the story line is basically the same. The world is created out of watery chaos when the divine champion defeats the raging sea.

This powerful mythic pattern has endured into the modern era in books like Herman Melville's *Moby Dick* and in movies such as *Jaws*. The climactic scene of that film closely follows the script of *Enuma Elish*. The hero, a police officer played by Roy Scheider, battles a supernaturally strong and relentless killer shark. His boat ravaged and sinking fast into the sea, Scheider finally manages to shove an oxygen tank into the killer shark's open mouth. Like a modern American Marduk, he shoots it with a rifle. And like Tiamat, the sea monster explodes. Order is restored. Life emerges victorious from the shattered pieces of watery chaos. Tourist season is saved.

Echoes of this ancient creation myth can be faintly heard in the Genesis 1 creation story, and more clearly in the short creation hymns in Isaiah 40:12, Psalm 33:6–7, and Job 38:8–11. But there are strong echoes of this ancient Near Eastern creation myth in the song of Moses and the Israelites (Exod. 15:1–18). Verse 8, for example, evokes Tiamat/Yamm and the successful battle of Marduk/Baal as it describes Yahweh's victory at the sea. "By the wind of your nostrils the waters piled up, the floods stood up like a heap; the deeps [*tehomot,*] congealed in the heart of the sea [*yam*]." Verses 10–11 build on the mythic imagery, portraying Yahweh in terms reminiscent of the praises heaped on the victorious storm god Marduk/Baal, enthroned as king of the gods after the battle with the sea: "You blew with your wind, the sea covered them. Majestic ones sank like lead in the waters. Who among the gods [ba'elim] compares with you, O Yahweh? Who compares with you, glorious in holiness, terrifying in splendor, performing wonders?"

A striking feature of the song is the target audience for the victory at the sea:

"The peoples heard, they trembled. A powerful pain seized the inhabitants of Philistia. Then the chiefs of Edom were terrified. The leaders of Moab were gripped with trembling. All the inhabitants of Canaan melted. Terror and dread fell upon them, by the greatness of your arm they became stiff as stone, until your people, O Yahweh, until the people you bought passed by." (vv. 14–16)

In the narrative version in chapter 14, Yahweh rescues Israel at the sea "so the Egyptians will know that I am Yahweh" (v. 4) and so Israel will "fear Yahweh" and "believe in Yahweh and his servant Moses" (v. 31). But in chapter 15, the victory is a terrifying sign for the nations Israel will encounter in its narrative future in the wilderness and when it enters the land of Canaan. The song, however, presents wilderness wandering and conquest as past events. In that moment of victory at the sea, past, present, and future collapse—Israel's sacred history is telescoped. The song's denouement is not escape at the sea, but the people's victorious entry into Yahweh's temple at Jerusalem. "You brought them and planted them on the mountain of your possession, the place you have chosen as your dwelling, O Yahweh, the sanctuary, my lord, that your hands have established. Yahweh will rule forever and ever!" (vv. 17–18). In this version, the victory at the sea finally is about the enthronement of Yahweh in Jerusalem and Israel's possession of Canaan, a visible sign of Yahweh's sovereign rule in the universe. As is often the case with Israel's sacred stories, the reader steps into a time warp, experiencing several "historical" moments all at once in the telling of the story. The victory at the sea is an enduring moment in Israel's history. The power of this liberating act of national "creation" is always immediate, ever accessible.

A much shorter, possibly older version, the song of Miriam and the women, follows the song of Moses. The chapter concludes with a brief story about God turning "bad" water good (vv. 22–27), paralleling God's creative work with the life-threatening waters of chaos, ordered and turned to good purpose in Genesis 1. This very short story reiterates the theme of Israel's "grumbling," already mentioned in earlier chapters, but more thoroughly developed in the wilderness traditions in the chapters that follow. It also provides the transition to the sabbath-manna story in chapter 16.

The manna story begins with Israel's complaint: "If only we had died at the hand of Yahweh in the land of Egypt when we were sitting at pots of meat and eating bread till we were full. You have surely brought us out to this wilderness to kill this whole assembly with famine!" In the Priestly view, Israel is playing with theological dynamite here, since the exodus is Yahweh's salvation-historical calling card, God's international debut. Israelites who long for the security of Egyptian bondage are not merely dimwitted cowards; they blaspheme Yahweh, the God who first and foremost liberates Hebrew slaves. The story thus begins on an ominous note.

Yahweh greets Israel's blasphemy with a cool head, however, promising bread and meat, but without the punitive tone found in the older version of the story in Numbers 11. There, an infuriated Yahweh promises meat "until it comes out your noses and you find it loathsome" (v. 20) and then buries the Israelite camp in quail carcasses three feet deep and a day's journey in every direction (v. 31). In Numbers, the gift of quail is a curse, not a blessing. By contrast, in the Exodus story, Yahweh's first words of response issue a challenge, but emphasize God's providential care: "I am raining bread from heaven for you. Let the people go out and gather a day's worth each day, so I can test them, whether they will follow my instruction or not" (v. 4).

In verse 19, Moses instructs Israel not to try to save the manna from one day to the next. The people's disobedience in verse 20 results in rotten food and an angry Moses. One can easily imagine that in an earlier version of this chapter, verses 19–21 provided the story's climax. Israel fails the test Yahweh sets up at the beginning of the episode.

In the final form of the narrative, however, the theme of Israel's unfaith is muted by the introduction of a second major theme in verse 5: sabbath. Verses 22–26 establish the peculiar characteristic of manna that, once every week, it yields twice as much and lasts twice as long as it does on the other days. Verses 27–30 underscore the point, as some of the people go out to gather on the seventh day and find no manna, prompting Yahweh and Moses to reiterate, with some irritation but no punishment, that the people need not worry about going hungry on the sabbath. Like sabbath at the world's creation, the first sabbath after Israel's national "creation" at the sea can be observed only because God lavishly provides more than enough for human life to survive and thrive—even in a hostile wilderness environment, unordered by agriculture. Sabbath, as portrayed in these stories, taps into the superabundant power of life present at the creation of the natural and national world. Sabbath observance is a statement of faith in God's reliable care as creator and eternal sovereign of the universe. Thus the sabbath theme connects with the concluding Priestly discourse on manna (vv. 31–35), where Yahweh commands Israel to preserve a sample of perishable manna as a sign for future generations—an act of faith that God is willing and able to ensure Israel's continued survival.

One other characteristic of sabbath-manna is important to note. The bread from heaven cannot be hoarded. In verse 16, Yahweh commands that each Israelite gather "as much of it as each needs to eat, an omer per person." Need is defined individually, not collectively, here. The welfare of the people is not measured as a long-term aggregate, Gross National Product, or average per capita income. Providential care is measured person by person. No individual Israelite will fall through the cracks. Verse 17 reports that different people collected different quantities: "Some gathered more, and some gathered less." But miraculously in verse 18, "when they measured with an omer, the ones with more had no surplus and the ones with less had no shortage. They all gathered exactly what they needed to eat!" God's gift is lavish. After all, God offers meat as well as bread and fills the basket of every single person, regardless of strength and ability. God's reliable, providential care is limited only by the actual needs of each individual Israelite.

Sabbath prosperity, the "fat" blessing of a benevolent world, is abundant, but not unlimited. Life's goods exist in finite, limited quantity.[12] Not scarce, but limited. God blesses generously, lavishly providing life abundant for each person under God's care, regardless of ability. But the surplus is limited by actual human need.

---

[12]See Bruce Malina's discussion of the notion of "limited goods" in ancient Mediterranean cultures, in *The New Testament World: Insights from Cultural Anthropology*, rev. ed. (Louisville: Westminster/John Knox, 1993), 90–116.

At issue is the very character of Israel's God as trustworthy and able. In the economy of the sabbath-manna story, hoarding is more than a simple case of rule-breaking. It is a fundamental act of disbelief. Greedy, excessive consumption is unfaith—unfaith rooted in the blasphemous fear that God is not what God has been revealed to be in the utterly gracious and powerful liberation of Hebrew slaves from Egypt: the Creator and sovereign of Israel and the whole world.

Social Location of the Sabbath Creation Stories

In their present forms, the Genesis 1 creation and Exodus 16 manna stories are products of Priestly writers concerned with reestablishing national life in Judah after Babylonian exile. The native Judean monarchy has ended. With the defeat of Babylon, royal control of Judah has passed to a culturally tolerant Persian imperial system that nevertheless makes the same economic and political demands that all ancient Near Eastern monarchies made. The political and cultural scene in and around Jerusalem changed dramatically when the Persians ousted the Babylonians. But the everyday lives of households in farms and villages were pretty much the same as they ever were.

As priests in the Persian-sponsored second temple, the Priestly writers probably had little interest in fomenting popular rebellion against the empire. In fact, their idyllic visions of sabbath world have a certain apolitical, "don't worry, be happy" ring to them. But ideas born in the context of social conflict may bounce around between classes and interest groups. And even the ideas of the ruling class necessarily reflect, in more or less distorted form, the interests of the ruled.

Whatever the class sympathies of the Priestly writers and editors of Genesis 1 and Exodus 16, the stories they wrote reflect specific interests of households struggling to survive the economic demands of ancient monarchy. In this sense, they share the underlying concerns of various jubilee and sabbath-year laws.

Biblical sabbath inhabits a narrative world that stands over against the world actually experienced by the working majority on whose labor the royal/imperial system was built. In the real monarchical world, farm and village households faced excessive work and periodic shortages of food and other subsistence goods. In the world of creation-sabbath (Genesis 1), all people, created in God's own image, could expect seven days of prosperity for six days of work, just as in the

Priestly vision of sabbath year they could expect seven years of produce for six years of planting (Lev. 25:19–22). In the real experience of Israelite and Jewish farmers, wealth and well-being were distributed hierarchically, the monarchy and its favored households controlling the lion's share, while the laboring majority lived constantly on the brink of debt slavery, property loss, and starvation. But in the narrative world of sabbath manna (Exod. 16), each gathers food according to ability, and each miraculously receives according to need. At day's end in sabbath world, there is neither shortage nor excess. No one lives off the exploited labor of others, and no one falls below that which is necessary for survival.

Sabbath anticipates and ritually celebrates an in-breaking world that reverses the severe conditions of peasant and village life under ancient monarchy. It rejects the "natural law" of scarcity, poverty, and excessive toil for the laboring majority alongside luxury, leisure, and excessive consumption for the court-connected few. It assumes instead a divinely sanctioned social and cosmic order characterized by social solidarity, natural abundance, and self-restraint. Sabbath world is like the world of sabbath year and jubilee, a world of release for those who struggle on the margins of royal economy, a vision of hope for a better life. In this sense, it is appropriate to think of sabbath day as a "little jubilee," a weekly celebration of the hoped-for world of release, where debts are forgiven, property returned, and slaves set free. Sabbath is both a prophetic critique of the royal status quo and a visionary call to build a better world. Sabbath is a foretaste of God's perfect rule.

Summary

Genesis 1 and Exodus 16 are Priestly stories of sabbath's origin. Genesis 1 ties sabbath to the creation of the world, grounding its observance in "natural law." Exodus 16 ties sabbath to the victory at the sea, grounding its observance in the "creation" of Israel, finally liberated from Egyptian slavery.

The two stories focus on themes of natural abundance, an excess of wealth that ensures universal blessing. The world is portrayed as fundamentally benevolent toward life, especially the life of human beings, created male and female in the image of God to exercise royal authority throughout the earth. In these stories, power and wealth are shared for the common good. Greed is condemned. And no one must go without.

The world of creation and wilderness manna is a peasant's dream world. These stories portray, not the world of real experience, but the world as it should be—a world where debt slaves are treated with the dignity due beings stamped with deity. It is a world of abundance, self-restraint, universally shared human power, and leisure, where wealth is distributed so that every single person has enough to eat. It is a world where everyone who is able works, and everyone gets what he or she needs to survive. Sabbath is rooted in the same concerns that ground the jubilee and sabbath-year laws. It is "a little jubilee," a weekly celebration anticipating a more just, humane world.

7

SABBATH AND HOUSEHOLD HOSPITALITY

M any sabbath passages highlight themes of social and economic justice and tie them to the nature of God and the character of God's relationship with the world. These ethical and theological implications of sabbath begin, however, with justice in the household.

Sabbath and Household Work

Remember the sabbath day, keeping it holy. Six days you may toil and do all your work, but the seventh day is sabbath for Yahweh your God. You must not do any work—neither you nor your son nor your daughter, your male slave nor your female slave, nor your animal, nor your resident alien who is in your gates. For six days Yahweh made the sky and the earth, the sea, and everything in them, and then rested on the seventh day. Therefore, Yahweh blessed the sabbath day and made it holy. (Exod. 20:8–11)

> Keep the sabbath day, keeping it holy just as Yahweh your
> God commanded you. Six days you may toil and do all your
> work, but the seventh day is sabbath for Yahweh your God.
> You must not do any work—neither you nor your son nor
> your daughter nor your male or female slave, nor your cattle
> nor your donkey nor any of your animals, nor your resident
> alien who is in your gates—so that your male and female
> slave will rest just like you do. Remember that you were a
> slave in the land of Egypt, and Yahweh your God brought
> you out from there, with a powerful hand and an outstretched
> arm. Therefore, Yahweh your God has commanded you to
> observe the sabbath day. (Deut. 5:12–15)

The sabbath law occupies a pivotal position in both versions of the
Decalogue (Ten Commandments), standing at the crux of theology
and ethics. The verses before the sabbath law address Israel's relationship with God, and the laws that follow regulate social relationships
within and between households. Sabbath grounds all those relationships in the identity of God as creator of the world and liberator of
Israel.

It is difficult to date the sabbath laws with any certainty. Most
sabbath references in the Pentateuch are located in blocks of material
that are generally thought to be exilic or postexilic. The seventh-year
and seventh-day law in Exodus 23:9–12, already discussed in an earlier chapter, is in a coherent literary unit, the Book of the Covenant,
which contains legal material found in much older documents from
the ancient world. Sabbath, however, is unique to Israel, as far as we
know. So there is no external point of reference by which to date the
sabbath laws in Exodus 23.

However old they are, the sabbath laws are consistent with each
other in their humanitarian rationale. Exodus 23:9–12 ties the seventh day to seventh-year release and grounds both observances in
concern for the life of the resident alien. The seventh-day law requires
Israelite householders to rest "so that your ox and donkey may rest,
and your homeborn slave may be revitalized, along with the resident
alien" (23:12). Sabbath is meant to revitalize the most vulnerable
workers in the household economy—the slave, the resident alien, and,
first of all, the farm animals. This striking provision for farm animals
is a function of humans' special charge to care for all the creatures of

the earth (Gen. 1:26–28). Humans, though important in the universe, are not the sole focus of God's attention. The entire creation stands in relationship with God, and nonhuman species are, like people, subject to God's ongoing care. But in the household economy of ancient Israel, rest for ox and donkey serves a human purpose as well. Requiring rest for beasts of burden effectively stops agricultural work. It is the ancient equivalent of closing the factory, locking up the office, hanging the "closed" sign on the business door, unplugging the phone, turning off the fax, and leaving the beeper in another room. Mandatory rest for ox and donkey means a day off for human laborers as well.

These passages appear to address large and wealthy households. Short versions of the sabbath laws such as Exodus 34:21 focus on the individual Israelite: "Six days you (singular) must toil, but on the seventh day you must rest. In plowing time and harvest, you must rest." But other passages, including the two versions of the Decalogue, expand the basic law to focus on people under the charge of a (prosperous) householder. "You must not do any work—neither you nor your son nor your daughter nor your male or female slave, nor your cattle nor your donkey nor any of your animals, nor your resident alien who is in your gates—so that your male and female slave will rest just as you do" (Deut. 5:14). Exodus 20:10 has virtually identical wording. The purpose of sabbath rest for "you" is that subordinate members of the household may enjoy rest "just as you do." "The boss" must rest so all the workers can rest.

This concern for justice within households may also underlie the curious ban on lighting fires in some versions of sabbath law. Exodus 35:2–3, for example, describes the seventh day as "a sabbath of complete rest [*shabbat shabbatôn*] for Yahweh" and treats violation as a capital crime. It concludes with the odd elaboration that "you must not light a fire in any of your dwellings on the sabbath day." The story of the man caught gathering firewood in the wilderness on sabbath day (Num. 15:32–36) is probably a *midrash* on the fire ban in Exodus 35. The man doubly violated sabbath, in his actual work of gathering and in his intended work of lighting a fire at home.

The punishment for the man's offense was death by stoning—an extreme sentence only rarely mentioned in connection with sabbath (Exod. 31:14, 35:2), but one with a logic deeply rooted in the basic rationale for sabbath observance. Some scholars see the ban on lighting fires as evidence that Israel's sabbath day originally was related to Mesopotamian "bad luck" days, around the time of the full moon, the *shabbatû*, on the thirteenth, fourteenth, or fifteenth of the month. According to this theory, sabbath observance originated in a superstition that it was bad luck to work outside or to light fires in or near the house on unlucky days.

That may be true, but there is another reason to ban the lighting of fires in the home on sabbath. Fires—at least the ones that required kindling—were lighted in or just outside the home for cooking. The fire ban ensures that Israelite householders will not expect the women to "fire up the oven" and cook, while the men enjoy sabbath-day rest. Sabbath knows no distinction of gender. It is a day of rest for women as well as men. The sabbath ban on lighting fires addresses the same concern that lies in the background of the sabbath-manna story and its warning not to gather manna on the seventh day. No one will be forced to work on sabbath. Male or female, slave or free—everyone is freed from toil. The man caught gathering firewood is not honored for his hard work because he works to violate the God-given rest due his wife and daughters on sabbath day. He violates household justice. Sabbath is a day of complete rest for the entire household, but especially for subordinates. The householder's respite is rest with a purpose—that everyone else in the household may enjoy relief from toil.

Sabbath violation is treated so seriously—capital punishment—because sabbath observance is a distinctive sign of Israel's covenant with Yahweh. The sign reflects the nature of God and the character of God's relationship with Israel. Sabbath is observed because Yahweh liberated Israelite slaves from Egypt (Deut. 5:15) and because God created a benevolent world (Exod. 20:11), teeming with life and lavish in its provision for human well-being.

Sabbath is a distinctive sign in the ancient Near East, because Yahweh is a distinctive deity, defining the divine-human relationship by rest, not work. This is a radical departure from the mythologies of Israel's ancient neighbors. In Mesopotamian myths, for example, human beings are created to do the gods' "grunt work." In the Babylonian creation myth, *Enuma Elish*, Marduk and Ea make human beings out of the blood of Tiamat's consort Kingu to do the gods' work: "Ea formed The Aborigines from Kingu's blood, Marduk set The Aborigines to work. Ea emancipated The Gods, The Wise created The

Aborigines. Marduk put The Aborigines to work and set The Gods free… Marduk ordered them to do The Gods' work."[1]

Yahweh, by contrast, created Israel by liberating the people from forced labor, buying their freedom from Egypt. In Israel's sacred story, humans, unlike the aborigines of the Babylonian myth, are created to rule the earth, not as slaves doing the gods' grunt work, but as kings and queens stamped with the image of God.

It is understandable—though chilling to modern sensibilities—that the Bible sometimes treats sabbath violation as a capital crime. Violating sabbath is blasphemy because it attacks the very character of Yahweh as redeemer of Israel, the God who frees rather than enslaves, who offers lavish blessing rather than endless toil. Sabbath is a deep symbol of Israel's intimate relationship with God. Violating sabbath is like throwing your wedding ring in the face of your spouse or burning your national flag. It is a serious and public statement of a permanent rupture. Yahweh alone among the deities of the ancient world offers rest as the distinguishing mark of the covenant people. Violating sabbath signals the end of this unique relationship.

Sabbath is Yahweh's distinctive mark, and it is the orientation point around which household justice in Israel coheres. Sabbath justice applies to all members of the household, but shows special concern for the welfare of the most vulnerable—the slave, the resident alien, the female. Sabbath is the great equalizer. Sabbath justice begins in the home but is the basis of a much broader social ethic.

Sabbath and Markets

Hear this, you who trample the poor and exterminate the lowly of the land, saying, "How long till the new moon passes, so we can sell grain, and the sabbath, so we can market wheat, shrinking the bushel,[2] expanding the buck,[3] and cheating with unbalanced scales, buying the helpless with silver and the poor for a pair of shoes, while we sell the sweepings of

---

[1]Victor H. Matthews and Don C. Benjamin, *Old Testament Parallels: Laws and Stories from the Ancient Near East* (New York/Mahwah, N.J.: Paulist Press, 1991), 115–17.

[2]I am taking liberties in translation here that border on paraphrase. An "ephah" is probably about half a bushel (cf. Ezek. 45:11, where an ephah is a tenth of a "homer," a "donkeyload," about 5–7 bushels).

[3]Another very loose translation. The word is "shekel."

the wheat." Yahweh swears by the arrogance of Jacob, "I will certainly never forget any of your deeds!" (Amos 8:4–7)

As we have seen, royal political economy put enormous strains on households in Israel and Judah. As families moved from subsistence farming toward more cash crops, markets became a more important, though still relatively small, part of the overall economy, particularly in cities. But markets brought potential for abuse. The wealthy came to market transactions with an inherent advantage over the poor. Several sabbath passages, particularly in prophetic books,[4] deal explicitly with economic injustice related to market exchanges.

Amos mentions sabbath only in 8:5, as part of a series of short oracles now woven together as a prophecy of destruction. This composite oracle is attached to the fourth of five "vision reports" (7:1–3; 7:4–6; 7:7–9; 8:1–3; 9:1–4) that structure the closing chapters of the book. The vision reports severely condemn the royal political economy and its temple apologists. They foretell increasingly severe punishment for Israel, as prelude to a surprising announcement of salvation (9:11–15) for a rebuilt, revitalized "Israel" (actually an expanded postexilic Judah), where God will raise "the booth of David that has fallen," repair its breaches, and raise its ruin "on that day" (9:11). The prophet's words thus function on different historical levels all at once. They address the harsh conditions of peasant life in royal Israel and Judah before destruction and exile. But in the final analysis, they point toward life in restored Judah after Babylonian exile has ended.

Chapter 8 continues the searing critique of royal religion and political economy in the previous three reports. The composite prophecy of doom is governed thematically by the vision (vv. 1–3) that introduces it. The accusation (vv. 4–6) focuses on the dispossessive power of markets and the debt system, highlighting the unjust intent of merchants and creditors by noting their impatient, though apparently scrupulous observance of new moon and sabbath. The accusation is followed by a fourfold announcement of judgment built on imagery of cosmic upheaval—earthquake (vv. 7–8), solar eclipse (vv. 9–10), famine (vv. 11–12), and drought (vv. 13–14). Social response to these cosmic disasters intensifies as the judgments proceed. The people mourn (v. 8) as if they lost an only son (v. 10), run frantically to and fro (v. 12), and finally collapse in a dead faint (v. 13), never to rise again (v. 14). Though described as a series of natural disasters and

---

[4]Isa. 1:13; 58:13; Jer. 17:21–27; Hos. 2:11; cf. Neh. 13:15–22.

increasingly severe social panic, the judgment's central point of impact is religious rather than ecological and economic. Festivals will be turned to mourning and songs to lamentation (v. 10), while the people experience a famine "of hearing the words of Yahweh" (v. 11).

The major themes are introduced in the vision report, verses 1–3:

> This is what my lord Yahweh showed me: something like a basket of summer fruit [*qayits*]! He said, "What are you seeing, Amos?" I said, "Something like a basket of summer fruit." And Yahweh said to me, "The end [*qets*] is coming to my people Israel. I will never again pass them by. Temple songs will wail in that day," declares my lord Yahweh. "Corpses will multiply, flung down everywhere. Hush!"

This fourth vision report is structured like the third (7:7–9) and parallels it thematically. Yahweh causes the prophet to see a basket of summer fruit or figs (*qayits*), bringing to mind the three previous visions (7:1, 4, 7) and Amos' self-description in 7:14, "I am a tender of fig-trees." Yahweh asks Amos, "What do you see?" Amos briefly answers, and Yahweh interprets the summer fruit (*qayits*) with a pun: "The end [*qets*] has come to my people Israel." The coming "end" parallels the "plumbline" set in the midst of Israel in the third vision (7:8). Both signal that Yahweh "will never again pass by them" (7:8; 8:2), that is, God will never again be revealed to Israel (cf. Exod. 33:18–23; 1 Kgs. 19:11–14). As "Isaac's high places will be desolated" and "Israel's sanctuaries put to the sword" (7:9), so now "temple songs will wail in that day" (8:3). As Yahweh "will rise up against Jeroboam's house with the sword" (7:9), so now "corpses will multiply, flung down everywhere" (8:3). From desolation to mourning, from Yahweh's declaration of war to the corpse-strewn battlefield, in each of its particulars, the fourth vision parallels the third and takes it one step further.

The temple stands at the center of Yahweh's concern. "Temple songs will wail in that day." The declaration is built on a double entendre. These are the songs of the *hêkal*, a word that may mean either "temple" or "palace." "Temple" is the usual translation. But in light of Amos' broader critique, the ambiguity of the Hebrew *hêkal* should be preserved in our reading of the text. This word strikes a chord rather than a single note. The temple (*hêkal*) acts in concert with political and economic players associated with the palace (*hêkal*), because it acts as a mouthpiece for the monarchy. The *hêkal* is the "court temple." The priesthood has danced to the beat of the king and turned a deaf ear to the outcry of the trampled poor. But Yahweh intends to bring this song and dance to an end. At Yahweh's prompting "on that day," the king and his priests will be singing a different tune. "Wailing" will replace their songs of joy.

In the vision's end, Yahweh offers a single, intriguing command: "Hush!" The subject is ambiguous. Who must hush? Temple singers, royal courtiers, Israel, the corpses, the prophet? Whoever else is covered by the order, Yahweh intends to "hush." There will be a "famine of hearing the words of Yahweh" (8:11).

Amos' critique of royal political economy and its cultic apologists is focused in the indictment (vv. 4–6), which draws a series of sharp contrasts to highlight the hypocrisy of royal Israel's religiously sanctioned political economy. The introductory call to attention, "Hear this!" calls to mind earlier oracles against Israel (3:1, 13; 4:1; 5:1) and the royal priest Amaziah (7:16). In each case, the oracle that follows the command to "Hear!" promises destruction because the ostentatious rich commit violence, robbery, and oppression against the poor (3:9–10, 15; 4:1; 5:7, 10–12). In 8:4 as well, the command to "Hear!" introduces a prediction of doom for royal Israel, whose political economy brings disaster to the economically vulnerable.

A pun brackets the indictment. Verse 4 addresses "those who trample the poor," the scrupulously pious market leaders, whose own self-incriminating words climax in their stated intention to "buy the poor for a pair of shoes" (v. 6). The better to trample you with, my dear!

The cruel irony of the image of the poor trampled underfoot for a pair of shoes is sharpened by the shifting focus of the accusation. The grain market is the metaphorical backdrop for the self-damning testimony of the accused. Their impatient, though rigorous, observance of commercial limitations imposed by new moon and sabbath barely restrains their eagerness to make money by unfairly marketing grain. But verse 6a shifts focus. Suddenly, it is not grain, but "the helpless" and "the poor" who are transacted at market by the greedy rich, who buy "the helpless with silver and the poor for a pair of shoes."

The quick change of subject back to grain in verse 6b is not an accidental transposition of clauses to be corrected,[5] but is a literary

---

[5]Some commentators would move this clause to the end of verse 5 for reasons of content and metrical balance. Cf. H. W. Wolff, *Joel and Amos*, Hermeneia; (Philadelphia: Fortress, 1977), 322, note h.

technique that embraces the subject of verse 6a, "the helpless and poor," within the metaphor of grain transactions in verse 5. The sudden shifts of subject prompt a rereading of the grain market imagery in the indictment as a whole. The "grain" and "wheat" that are traded, trampled underfoot, swept up, and resold are simultaneously agricultural produce and human lives. These images refer both to the dispossessive power of market agriculture and to the peasant farmers themselves, who are squeezed between the subsistence agriculture they need to survive and the "surplus" production they must pursue to meet tax and debt requirements of royal political economy. Like "sweepings of wheat" that spill unnoticed on the ground in the normal course of trade and are trampled underfoot, the helpless poor are the refuse of the royal system. They are valuable at all only because the wealthy are so greedy that they even sweep up the spillage and package it for sale.

A second important pun spans verses 4 and 5: "Those who exterminate [*lashebbît*] the lowly of the land" (v. 4b) are the ones who are anxious for the sabbath (*hashshabbat*) to pass so they can sell grain and cheat customers (v. 5b). "Exterminate" translates a verbal form of the Hebrew word that means "sabbath" when it appears as a noun. It means "to cause to cease, to bring to an end." By their buying and selling practices, greedy marketeers are doing to the lowly of the land what sabbath does to work, putting an end to them, causing them to cease.

The irony of the merchants' self-incriminating statement works only if new moon and sabbath have a rationale similar to the one in the Pentateuch's sabbath passages discussed earlier in this chapter. As Exodus 20:8–11, 23:12, and Deuteronomy 5:12–15 make clear, sabbath, like sabbath year and jubilee (Exod. 23:10–11; Deut. 15:1–18; Lev. 25—26), provides relief for the economically vulnerable, especially menial laborers and slaves. Read against the rationale of these passages, "causing to cease" (*lashebbît*), that is, "making a sabbath," should bring compassionate relief to the lowly of the land. Ironically and tragically, the powerful use sabbath as a weapon against the weak. Instead of making a sabbath *for* the poor, the obsessively pious rich make a sabbath *of* the poor, bringing them to an end.

The merchants of agricultural produce and human flesh are not condemned for technical violations of sabbath law. These tramplers of the poor are the very ones who "transgress" at Bethel by oppressing the poor while bringing their sacrifices every morning and their tithes every three days, who offer up thank offerings of unleavened bread, and who mandate freewill offerings (4:4–5). They do not violate laws of ritual observance and cultic purity. They keep them to the point of absurdity, even while they undermine the poor. It is not surprising, then, that they follow the letter of sabbath law in spite of their impatience with the loss of revenue.

Three other biblical books contain possible restrictions on sabbath commerce. Isaiah 58:13 urges the people to "remove your foot from sabbath, doing your own business on my holy day." "Doing your own business" may include commerce, but it probably means more than that—something like arrogant self-absorption or "doing your own thing." This seems to be the idea in the final clause of the verse, where God urges the greedy to "honor [sabbath] more than making your own way, more than finding your own interest"—or perhaps, "finding what's in it for you." Overall, Isaiah 58 is concerned with relief for oppressed workers (v. 5), liberty for enslaved debtors (v. 6), food for the hungry (vv. 7, 10–11), clothing for the naked (v. 7), and housing for the homeless (v. 7). It is certain that verse 13's sabbath concern is broadly economic, and not strictly limited to bad commercial practices.

A clearer parallel to Amos 8:5 is Nehemiah's ban on sabbath commerce in rebuilt Jerusalem (Neh. 10:31; 13:15–22). It may be, however, that Nehemiah's order is a special purity law for Jerusalem as Judah's officially designated "holy city," the home of the provincial temple. This may also be the case in Jeremiah 17:21–27 where the people of Jerusalem are warned not to "bear a burden on the sabbath" or "bring it in by the gates of Jerusalem." Special sabbath regulations for Jerusalem before Babylonian exile or during the Persian restoration would be unsurprising, since it was common for temple cities to operate by different laws to maintain a higher level of purity in the precincts of sacred shrines.[6]

This may be the sense of Amos 8:5 as well, assuming the narrative setting is Bethel, a city of "the royal sanctuary and temple of the realm" (7:13). If this reading is correct, the impatience of new moon- and sabbath- observant merchants identifies them as inhabitants of

---

[6]See Weinfeld's chapter "Privileges and Freedoms of Temple Cities," *Social Justice*, 97–132, for numerous examples in Israel and the ancient Near East.

the temple city and, therefore, closely connected with the royal political-religious system there. These are friends and officials of the king, who represent the interests, prerogatives, and abuses of royal political economy, given religious sanction by the temple.

Amos 8:5 turns on a fundamental misunderstanding of sabbath. The privileged wealthy scrupulously observe the sabbath ban on commerce just as they obsessively keep the requirements of temple purity. But they completely misunderstand the significance of sabbath relief. By trampling the poor, the pious allies of the crown violate sabbath, even while religiously taking a daylong pause. Sabbath is a day of rest, but more fundamentally, it is a call to economic justice.

Sabbath and Hospitality

You must take choice flour and bake twelve cakes of it, two-tenths [of an ephah] to each cake. And you must place them in two rows, six to a row, on the pure table before Yahweh. You must put pure frankincense with the rows. It will be for the bread a flaming memorial to Yahweh. Every sabbath day, [Aaron] must arrange them before Yahweh, continuously from the Israelites, an everlasting covenant. It will be for Aaron and his descendants. They will consume it in the holy place, because it is supremely holy to him, from the fires of Yahweh, an everlasting portion. (Lev. 24:5–9)

Sabbath is usually portrayed in the Bible as a household observance with deep theological and ethical significance, but no distinctive rituals and liturgies. It is a day of relief from labor, not a day of formal worship. Sabbath is regularly observed in households throughout Israel without benefit of priest or king. But in some late passages, sabbath is associated with temple and sacrifice,[7] and in several places it is mentioned as part of a triad of sacred festivals: new moon, sabbath, and appointed feasts.[8]

As we saw in the brief discussion of sabbath's origins in the first chapter, the task of deciphering the sabbath as a cultic festival is

---

[7]Lev. 19:30; 26:2; Num. 28:9–10; 1 Chr. 23:31; 2 Chr. 8:13; 31:3; Neh. 10:33; Ezek. 45:17; 46:1–2; Lam. 2:6.

[8]1 Chr. 23:31; 2 Chr. 2:4; 8:13; 31:3; Neh. 10:33; Isa. 1:13; Ezek. 45:17; Hos. 2:11.

complicated by the fact that "sabbath" in the Bible may not always refer to seventh-day rest. Indeed, its frequent association with a new-moon celebration[9] suggests that "sabbath" as a First Temple cultic festival may have been a lunar celebration of some sort, perhaps a full moon festival, linked with divine election of the royal dynasty.[10] Whatever the original meaning of "sabbath," its association with the sanctuary's "bread of the presence" (Lev. 24:8; 1 Chr. 9:32; 2 Chr. 2:4; Neh. 10:33) ties sabbath to a theological understanding that portrays God as hospitable host.

The bread of the presence was kept in front of the throne of Yahweh, just outside the holiest place in the sanctuary. Narratives about the tabernacle are found especially in the last half of Exodus and in parts of Leviticus and Numbers. All these books took their current shape long after the first Jerusalem temple was destroyed and the Second Temple was well under way. Their descriptions of the tabernacle are based on the floor plan of the temple.

An oblong wooden box, the "ark of the covenant," sat in the most holy place at the center of the sanctuary. The ark served as "footstool" to the "mercy seat," a slab of pure gold that sat above the ark. Two golden statues called "cherubim," winged sphinxes with animal bodies and human heads, were attached to the sides of the mercy seat. Their outstretched wings touched at the back and pointed forward at the sides. Yahweh was thought to sit between the cherubim, just above the mercy seat (Isa. 6; Ezek. 1—2).

A screen separated the ark from other furniture in the holy room at the center of the sanctuary. A seven-lamp lampstand was in front of the screen to the south. Opposite the lampstand to the north sat a table[11] with bowls and plates where the bread of the presence was placed each sabbath. The bread was consumed, not by fire offering to Yahweh, but by priestly representatives who ate it on the people's behalf.[12]

The bread of the presence was an offering, prepared by the people and placed before Yahweh's throne. But it was an offering from God

---

[9]2 Kgs. 4:23; 1 Chr. 23:31; 2 Chr. 2:4; 8:13; 31:3; Neh. 10:33; Isa. 1:13; 66:23; Ezek. 45:17; 46:1; 46:3; Hos. 2:11; Amos 8:5; Col. 2:16.

[10]2 Kgs. 11:5–9 = 2 Chr. 23:4–8; 2 Kgs. 16:18; Ezek. 45:17; 2 Chr. 2:4; 8:13; 31:3; Lam. 2:8. Also note Num. 29:6; 1 Sam. 20:5, 18, 24, 27; 1 Chr. 23:31; Ezra 3:5; Neh. 10:33; Ps. 81:3; Ezek. 46:1–12, where new-moon celebration is associated with the royal house and/or the temple.

[11]Exod. 25:23–30; 26:35; 35:13; 40:22–23; Num. 4:7–8.

[12]Lev. 24:5–9 describes the preparation and consumption of the bread (cf. 1 Chr. 9:32; 2 Chr. 2:4; 8:13; Neh. 10:33).

to the people. Like manna in the wilderness, the bread was a sign of God's hospitality to Israel, God's presence and protection for vulnerable travelers outside their zone of clan support. The holy precinct was furnished as a banquet hall with God seated as host, and the people, through their priestly representatives, invited as guests to dine. Yahweh is thus portrayed as the ideal hospitable host, welcoming Israel as Abraham and Sarah lavishly welcomed Yahweh and the angels at the oaks of Mamre (Gen. 18:1–15), baking loaves in excessive proportions, with the finest flour (v. 6).

At the table of the bread of the presence, God meets the people as gracious host, ever-present caregiver to a wandering people, unsettled and uncertain of what tomorrow may hold. The ritual preparation, placement, and consumption of the bread of the presence every sabbath dramatically represent the character of God and the quality of divine-human relationship revealed in stories such as sabbath-manna in Exodus 16. In wilderness manna and tabernacle bread, Yahweh is portrayed as generous provider and willing protector of the vulnerable, the ideal and honorable host who offers hospitality to those in need. Every sabbath is a renewal of this never-ending cycle of care.

A House of Prayer for All the Peoples

Thus says Yahweh: "Keep justice, and do righteousness! For my salvation is about to come, and my righteousness to be revealed! Happy is the one who does this, the mortal who holds it fast, keeping sabbath, not profaning it, and keeping his hand from doing any evil. Let the foreigner, the one joined to Yahweh, not say, 'Yahweh will certainly separate me from his people.' Let the eunuch not say, 'Look, I am a dry tree!' For thus says Yahweh to the eunuchs who keep my sabbaths and choose what pleases me and who hold fast to my covenant, I am giving you, within my house and within my walls, a power and name (*yad washem*) better than sons and daughters. I will give them an everlasting name that will not be cut off! And the children of the foreigner who is joined to Yahweh to minister to him and to love the name of Yahweh, to be a servant for him, everyone who keeps sabbath, not profaning it and holding fast to my covenant. And the ones whom I bring to my holy mountain and whom I make happy in my house of prayer, their burnt offerings and their sacrifices will be accepted on my altar, because my house will be called a house of prayer for all the peoples. Yahweh, the one who gathers the exiles of Israel, declares: I will still gather others besides the gathered ones." (Isa. 56:1–8)

The hospitality of God symbolized in the bread of presence is expanded in this early postexilic passage to embrace people outside of Israel, including those who are explicitly excluded from temple worship by other scriptures. In this prophet's vision of the rebuilt Jerusalem temple, even former enemies of Israel will be welcome. Though these verses are probably written later by a different hand, they reflect the visionary hope of Isaiah 2:2–4 (//Mic 4:1–3):

> In the days to come, the mountain of Yahweh's house will be established as the chief of the mountains. It will be raised up above the hills, and all the nations will stream to it. Many peoples will come and say, "Come, let us go up to the mountain of Yahweh, to the house of the God of Jacob that he may teach us his ways and we may walk in his paths."…And they will beat their swords into plowshares, and their spears into pruning hooks. Nation will not lift sword against nation. And they will no longer learn war.

Both passages dream of an ideal future where hostilities end and all the world's people find redemption and purpose in the universal embrace of Israel's God.

Isaiah 56 introduces a section of the book that scholars have dubbed "Third Isaiah." The book of Isaiah has a long and complex literary history. Its oracles and narratives span at least two centuries and are shaped by a variety of authors and editors. The imprints of different historical periods can be seen throughout the book, from the opening chapter on, but it takes a dramatic narrative turn at chapter 40. The first thirty-nine chapters contain oracles and narratives related to the life and ministry of Isaiah ben Amoz, a Jerusalem temple prophet who advised a series of Judean kings in the late 700s B.C.E., during the early years of Judah's lopsided alliance with the imperial superpower Assyria. Though some of the material dates from Isaiah's time, these chapters took their present shape and arrangement long after Isaiah died. Nevertheless, the narrative world they inhabit is the world of "invincible" royal Jerusalem in the late 700s. And the starring human role belongs to Isaiah.

Isaiah disappears as a character in chapter 40 and never returns. The reader suddenly finds herself in a very different narrative setting. "Comfort, O comfort my people says your God," the now anonymous prophet proclaims. "Speak tenderly to Jerusalem and cry to her that she has served her term and her penalty is paid, that she has received from Yahweh's hand double for all her sins." The next eleven chapters—scholars call this unit "Second Isaiah"—speak to Judeans in Babylonian exile, nearly two centuries after the first Isaiah prophesied. Jerusalem is now in ruins, the temple a pile of rubble. The once powerful leaders of Judah are in exile and in theological crisis. Now, almost 50 years after the Babylonians destroyed Jerusalem and deported its royal court, Second Isaiah discerns, in the rise of the Persian empire, Yahweh working to rescue the exiles and take them home again to Jerusalem.

The book takes another, less dramatic turn in Isaiah 56. From here to the end of the book, the focus shifts from returning to rebuilding. The questions that occupy these chapters focus on starting Jerusalem temple worship again and defining the nature of the restored worshiping community. There is also a discernible shift from the coherent and generally optimistic message of Second Isaiah. Chapters 56—66 (scholars call this final section of the book, "Third Isaiah") seem more ambivalent than Second Isaiah does. In Third Isaiah the mood swings suddenly and dramatically from hope to despair, and the message from promise to judgment and back again. The tenor and content of these chapters is so erratic that many scholars see Third Isaiah, not as the work of a single prophet, but as a collection of oracles by several postexilic prophets.

It is possible, however, to discern an overarching pattern. Third Isaiah celebrates the Jerusalem temple on Mount Zion, restored and vindicated before the nations. And the prophet envisions a universal community of worship gathering there to honor Yahweh, the God who liberates Israel from Babylonian captivity.

"As a mother comforts her child," Yahweh says to the international congregation about to gather in Jerusalem, "so I will comfort you" (66:13). "You will nurse and be carried on [Jerusalem's] arm, and be bounced on her knees" (66:12). "I am coming to gather all nations and languages" (66:18). "From new moon to new moon, from sabbath to sabbath, all flesh will come to worship me" (66:23).

Universal welcome at Yahweh's house is offered as divine *derôr*, a royal declaration of release for captives and debt slaves. "The spirit of my lord Yahweh is upon me, because Yahweh has anointed me, has sent me to bring good news to the oppressed, to bind up the brokenhearted, to proclaim liberty (*derôr*) for captives, to open the eyes of prisoners, to proclaim the year of Yahweh's favor" (61:1–2).

The first eight verses of 56 speak of a rebuilt Jerusalem temple that will throw the doors wide open and offer unprecedented hospitality: "My house will be called a house of prayer for all the peoples!" (56:7). In the new era that follows the fall of Babylon, God will gather not only the exiles of Israel, but other outcasts as well (56:8). Eunuchs and foreigners, formerly banned from the temple by their sexual and political status, will find welcome in the restored temple, as long as they "keep my sabbaths and hold fast my covenant."

The curious inclusion of "eunuchs" overturns an explicit ban in Deuteronomy 23:1 (cf. Lev. 21:20). Though perhaps related to the notion that physical deformities made one impure,[13] the eunuch ban in Deuteronomy served a political purpose as well.

The deuteronomic code began to take shape around the time of King Josiah, toward the end of the Judean monarchy, as part of a cultural revolution that followed the collapse of Assyrian imperial power in Judah. Deuteronomic reformers sympathetic to Josiah's nationalist, anti-imperialist policies were committed to erasing foreign (i.e., Assyrian) influence in Judah's internal affairs. Since "church" and "state" were inseparable, and the Jerusalem temple was closely tied to royal political power, it was important that Assyrian officers be kept from meddling in religious affairs.[14]

Unlike Judean court officials, high-ranking Assyrian bureaucrats often were eunuchs. Castration served a practical political purpose.

---

[13]This is almost certainly the case in the Leviticus passage, as the broader context (21:17–23) makes clear.

[14]According to the deuteronomistic account of his reign, King Ahaz, the first Judean king to submit to Assyrian imperial authority, overhauled the Jerusalem temple immediately after he sealed the treaty with the empire. He made major changes in temple architecture, furnishing, and practice "because of the king of Assyria" (2 Kings 16:18). For a thorough discussion of the scholarship on deuteronomic reform and its relationship to anti-Assyrian sentiments in Judah, see Richard H. Lowery, *The Reforming Kings: Cult and Society in First Temple Judah,* Journal for the study of the Old Testament Supplement 120 (Sheffield: JSOT Press, 1991).

Assyrian officials who kept the treasuries or served as ambassadors, provincial governors, and the like could become enormously powerful, making them potential threats to the king. Because producing an heir to the throne was politically essential for stable rule, the castrated bureaucrat, however politically powerful, was effectively neutralized as a potential usurper. The operation was performed on adults, but also on boys who had been set aside for royal service at an early age.

Deuteronomy's ban on eunuchs in the temple sought to limit foreign imperial influence in the religious-political affairs of Judah. When Isaiah 56 lifts the ban for those foreigners and eunuchs "who keep my sabbaths and hold fast my covenant," it announces the advent of a new era, an age of unprecedented possibility. In this new day of restoration, Israel's imperial oppressors no longer threaten. They exchange the power of sword and spear for the plowshares of sabbath-keeping faith in Israel's God, who gathers Israel and other outcasts as well. Ancient, deep-seated hostilities are overcome in the universal hospitality of God.

Summary

Biblical sabbath-keeping, though rooted in theological notions about the nature of God and God's covenant with Israel, has a fundamentally humanitarian rationale. Sabbath justice begins in the household in just relationships between male and female, old and young, subordinates and "bosses." Sabbath rest is, above all, relief for the household's most vulnerable members.

The household ethic at the root of sabbath is the foundation of a broader social-economic ethic expressed in prophetic condemnations of the royal political economy, such as those found in Amos. This prophetic critique makes clear that sabbath has a distinctively economic dimension. It is a matter of justice, not simply a pious holiday. In fact, the failure to attend to the needs of the vulnerable negates the value of "technical" observances of sabbath-day rest. Sabbath without justice is blasphemy.

Finally, the economics of sabbath reflect the character of Israel's God, symbolized in sabbath observance associated with the bread of the presence. Yahweh is envisioned as the ideal housekeeper and host, extending generous hospitality to Israel, depicted as vulnerable travelers cut off from access to the normal networks of social support. In later passages, such as Isaiah 56, Yahweh's hospitality to Israel is portrayed as universally expansive, embracing even those formerly considered enemies and explicitly excluded from the community of blessing.

8

SABBATH MADE FOR HUMANS

In the synoptic gospels, the sabbath appears explicitly only a handful of times. It plays a role in the passion narrative, perhaps reflecting a presynoptic tradition that Jesus was crucified on Friday, the "day of preparation" for the sabbath, and that his empty tomb was discovered on "the first day of the week," the day immediately following the sabbath. It is hard to know whether this reflects historical memory or a theological concern of Mark or pre-Markan Christian communities. In any case, sabbath lies at the center of the passion narratives, though none of the gospels makes explicit theological hay out of it.

In the synoptics and John, sabbath lies at the heart of an ongoing rabbinical dispute between Jesus and the Pharisees. The stated question is whether healing is permitted on the sabbath, but the deeper issue is the character of God revealed in sabbath observance. The synoptics link two stories: Jesus' disciples picking grain on the sabbath and Jesus healing the man with a withered hand. Two other stories, the healing of the woman with a debilitating spirit and of the man who had dropsy, are found only in Luke. The sabbath is the occasion for Jesus' inaugural sermon in Luke, an episode that explicitly

123

links Jesus' ministry with liberty in Isaiah 61. Finally, several of Jesus' teachings, including the "don't worry" sayings and the Lord's Prayer, reflect sabbath, sabbath-year, and jubilee themes.

Jesus' Ministry: Hospitality and Healing

"The Sabbath is given to you, but you are not servants of the Sabbath. We should disregard one Sabbath for the sake of saving the life of a person, so that he may observe many Sabbaths." (*Mechilta Shabbata I*)

Now on the sabbath, he was going through the grainfields. As they made their way, his disciples began to pluck heads of grain. The Pharisees said to him, "Hey! Why are they doing what is not permissible on the sabbath?" And he said to them, "Haven't you people ever read what David did when he and his companions had need and were hungry? How he went into the house of God when Abiathar was high priest, and he ate the bread of the presence—which cannot be eaten, except by the priests—and he gave some to his companions?" Then he said to them, "The sabbath was made for the human, not the human for the sabbath. Therefore, the human being is lord even of the sabbath."

Then he went back into the synagogue. Now there was a man there who had a withered hand. They watched him carefully to see whether he would heal him on the sabbath, so they might bring charges against him. He said to the man who had the withered hand, "Come to the center!" Then he said to them, "Is it permissible to do good on the sabbath or to do harm?" They were silent. Angrily looking around at them, grieved at their hard-heartedness, he said to the man, "Stretch out the hand!" And he stretched it out, and his hand was restored! Then the Pharisees went immediately and plotted against him with the Herodians, how to ruin him. (Mark 2:23—3:6)

Mark provides what has become, for many, the definitive (and basically negative) Christian teaching on sabbath observance. The story of Jesus' disciples picking grain on the sabbath is repeated with slight variations in Matthew 12:1–8 and Luke 6:1–5. It has no parallel in the Gospel of Thomas. In all three synoptics, it is connected with the story of the man with a withered hand (Mark 3:1–6; Matt. 12:9–14; Luke 6:6–11).

These are the final episodes in a series of five controversy stories that begin in Mark 2:1. This unit is structured chiastically,[1] the five episodes arranged in an A-B-C-B-A pattern. The last episode mirrors the first, the second-to-the-last mirrors the second, and the middle episode stands alone. This literary technique focuses the reader's attention on the unparalleled episode in the middle, which contains the larger unit's main point and provides its interpretive key.

In each episode, Jesus' disputed behavior functions as a prophetic "sign-act," a symbolic demonstration of a divinely revealed truth. His actions illustrate his teachings about the nature and authority of "the human being," an enigmatic phrase often translated, "the son of Man." "The human being" here may be a generic reference to humanity, the common sense rendering of the phrase in Hebrew and Aramaic (cf. Ps. 8:4; Ezek. 2:1; Dan. 7:13). Or, as many scholars think, it may be Jesus' self-designating title in Mark. Even so, the title is grounded in Jesus' role as representative human, a role especially revealed in his rejection, suffering, and death (Mark 8:31; 9:12; 14:21, 41). So the practical difference between the two possible readings may not be all that great. As "the human being," Jesus participates fully in the humanity of all people. The "authority of the human being" is the authority of Jesus, but it is also the authority of all human beings. This double thrust of the term is illustrated most clearly by Jesus' comment in 2:27–28: "The sabbath is made for the human, not the human for the sabbath. Therefore, the human being is lord even of the sabbath." "The human being" is Jesus in his representative role, but it is also humanity in general. The human being is lord of the sabbath because sabbath was made for human beings.

The first and last episodes in this series of controversies are healing stories that address the authority of the human being over matters of moral purity and religious obligation. In the first story (2:1–12), Jesus heals a man who cannot walk. The dispute is sparked by Jesus' announcement that the man's sins are forgiven. Jesus performs the healing as a sign-act to show that "the human being has the authority

---

[1]The term "chiasm" is derived from the Greek letter "chi," roughly shaped like an "x." In a "chiastic" literary structure, the second half "mirrors" the first half. The two halves turn on the "pivotal" middle, literally and figuratively the "central point" of the literary unit.

on earth to forgive sins" (v. 10). In the last story (3:1–6), Jesus heals the man with a disabled hand. The healing illustrates the principle that "the sabbath is made for the human" (2:27–28). Jesus focuses the issue in a rhetorical question to the synagogue crowd: "Is it permissible to do good on the sabbath or to do harm?" Jesus answers his own question by ordering the man to "stretch out your hand!"

The second and second-to-the-last episodes deal with food. Table rules are central to cultural self-definition in every place and time, but they were especially important in the Greco-Roman world. Cultural distinctiveness in this multicultural empire was marked by how, what, and with whom one ate. Disputes about preparation and consumption of food were really arguments about cultural identity. And maintaining cultural identity was especially important for subject peoples politically and economically dominated by Rome.

In the second episode (2:13–17), Jesus scandalizes his opponents, "the scribes of the Pharisees," by sitting at a table with culturally marginal people, "tax collectors and sinners"—people whose morally questionable work and loose behavior put them in regular contact with impure outsiders, especially the Romans. Cultural impurity, like a virus or harmful bacteria, could be transferred by touch, so Jesus' reckless table manners put him at risk of infection. Though baffling to his opponents, Jesus' bizarre behavior at the house of Levi the tax collector[2] illustrates the nature of his ministry: "Those who are well have no need of a doctor, but those who are sick do. I have come to call not the righteous, but sinners" (v. 17). In the second-to-last episode (2:23–28), Jesus offends his opponents by allowing his disciples to pluck grain on the sabbath. Their questionable behavior illustrates the principle that "sabbath was made for the human" (v. 27).

The action in the central episode (2:18–22) of the controversy stories is prompted by the observation that Jesus and his disciples do not fast like the disciples of John and the Pharisees do (v. 18). Jesus' response turns on the metaphor of a banquet, an image of the divine-human relationship well-rooted in biblical tradition (Ps. 23:5–6; Isa. 55:1–5, etc.). Images of fertility, prosperity, and joyful celebration fill Jesus' rhetoric, reminding the reader of the lavish abundance promised in the creation-sabbath and sabbath-manna stories in Genesis and Exodus. The banquet is a wedding feast, a celebration of God's

---

[2]"Levi" is a priestly name. That "Levi" is a "tax collector" sets up an absurd clash of expectations. "Pure" and "impure" collide in the very name of the dinner host.

blessing at creation: "Be fruitful, become numerous!" The joy is that of friends of the groom on this day of new beginnings and hope for future generations. "The wedding guests cannot fast while the bridegroom is still with them, can they?" Jesus asks.

The image of lavish banquet sets up the pivotal saying in verses 21–22: "No one sews a piece of unshrunk cloth on an old cloak, lest the patch pull away from it, the new from the old, and a worse tear is made. And no one puts new wine into old wineskins, lest the wine burst the skins and the wine is lost, along with the skins. You put new wine into fresh wineskins." The ministry of Jesus heralds a new age, bursting with lavish abundance that cannot be contained in the social and religious forms of the old. The extravagant bounty of the new age requires new, more expansive wineskins.

The generous abundance of the new age provides the interpretive key to the other stories in this series of disputes. The authority of the human being to forgive sins, to master sabbath, to eat with the unclean, and to distribute freely the temple's holy bread springs from the abundant overflow of a new age that cannot be contained in the wineskins of the old. Through the lens of lavish abundance in this new era, the sabbath dispute stories come into focus.

The first of the two sabbath stories (2:23–28) sets the narrative stage for the second (3:1–6). Plucking grain frames sabbath healing by setting sabbath in the context of the gleaning and agricultural sabbath-year traditions (Exod. 23:9–12). Sabbath, "made for the human," is above all an occasion of social justice, a hopeful celebration of full and prosperous life for all.

The story begins on the sabbath, with Jesus going through grain fields. It starts with Jesus alone, but the cast immediately expands: "As they made their way, his disciples began to pluck heads of grain." The narrative entourage quickly grows larger still. Traveling alongside Jesus' rabbinical students are his rabbinical rivals, "the Pharisees," who dutifully engage the Rabbi in an argument about his disciples' behavior and the proper interpretation of Torah. Responding to their criticism that his disciples have violated sabbath law by picking grain, Jesus cites David's eating the bread of the presence (1 Sam. 21:1–6) as legal precedent for their action. He concludes by asserting that "sabbath was made for the human, and not the human for the sabbath. Therefore, the human being is lord even of the sabbath" (Mark 2:27–28). Matthew and Luke drop the first sentence (v. 27; cf. Matt 12:8;

Luke 6:5). Only Mark says that "sabbath was made for the human, not the human for the sabbath."

The dispute between Jesus and his rabbinical opponents is not whether to observe sabbath, but how to observe it. The Pharisees apparently interpret the disciples' plucking of grain in light of Exodus 34:21, which explicitly forbids agricultural work on the sabbath: "In plowing time and harvest, you must rest!" The more fitting association, however, is the gleaning tradition (Lev. 19:9–10; 23:22; Deut. 24:19–21; Ruth 2), and the sabbath and sabbath-year laws in Exodus 23:9–12, which ground seventh day and seventh year in economic support for the resident alien. Jesus' disciples pluck grain, not as householders who own the crop and have the right to sell it, but as the economically vulnerable who have a God-given right to take what they need to survive.

Jesus underlines the connection with gleaning and sabbath-year traditions by interpreting his disciples' action through the story of David eating the bread of the presence (1 Sam. 21:1–9). There are two apparent errors of detail in his telling of the David story. (Matthew and Luke correct these "mistakes" in Mark.) In verse 26, Jesus says that David "entered the house of God, when Abiathar was high priest." According to 1 Samuel, the sanctuary was not a "house of God" and Abiathar was not the high priest there.

In Hebrew, "house of God" (*bêt 'el*) is a technical term that means "temple." The Yahweh shrine at Nob, where the David story takes place, is not a "house of God"—at least not according to the Deuteronomistic History (Deuteronomy—Kings), which insists that no Yahweh temple existed before Solomon built the temple in Jerusalem (2 Sam. 7:2, 5–7; 1 Kgs. 8:16). The only exception to this iron-clad rule is found in the first three chapters of Samuel, where the shrine at Shiloh is described as a "house of Yahweh" and a "temple" (*hêkal*; cf. Jer. 7:12–14). This exception serves a critical narrative purpose, however, associating the disastrous fate of Shiloh with the subsequent fate of Jerusalem and tying the story of Hannah, Eli, and Samuel to the tragic story of Israel's monarchy yet to come.[3] Besides this exceptional case, only the shrine in Jerusalem is called a "house of God."

---

[3]The messianic undercurrent springs to the surface at the climax of Hannah's song, celebrating the promised birth of Samuel: "Yahweh will judge the ends of the earth and give strength to his king and boost the power of his messiah" (1 Sam. 2:10).

Yet Mark's Jesus speaks of David's entering "the house of God" to eat the bread of the presence. It is, of course, possible that Jesus uses the term more loosely than the Hebrew Scriptures do, or that he cites a variant tradition, that he simply gets it wrong. But whatever the reason, identifying the story with "the house of God" identifies it with the temple.

The other error in Jesus' telling of the David story is its saying that it happened "when Abiathar was high priest." According to 1 Samuel, Ahimelech was the priest who let David eat the bread of the presence. Later, King Saul executes Ahimelech and his family for helping David. Abiathar is the only member of the priestly family who escapes. He joins David and eventually becomes one of two chief priests of the House of David (2 Sam. 20:25).[4] Accidental or not, Jesus' mistakes cast the episode at Nob as a story about Davidic monarchy and Jerusalem temple.

The story in 1 Samuel is prompted by the immediate need of David, fleeing Saul: "I have arranged to meet my boys here. We need food!" The priest Ahimelech is concerned about the purity of David and his comrades. David assures the priest that they are not unclean from sexual contact and that their cultic vessels are pure. The priest's concern about David and his companions parallels that of Jesus' opponents in the dispute (Mark 2:13–17) that mirrors the plucking grain narrative. At the house of Levi the tax collector, Jesus' opponents are worried about Jesus' purity because he eats with "tax collectors and sinners." At Nob, the priest is worried about the cultic purity of David's gang, whose life at the social and political margins makes them likely to be ritually unclean. The underlying issue in both stories is cultic and cultural purity.

In Jesus' view, however, the material needs of the hungry and the superabundance of the new age frame the issue differently. In the Samuel story, David assures Ahimelech that he and his comrades are not ritually impure and, therefore, will not defile the bread. The purity

---

[4] Zadok is the other. Second Samuel 8:17 mistakenly reverses the names of the father and the son, saying that "Ahimelech son of Abiathar" was David's priest. Perhaps this is the source of Jesus' confusion in Mark. Every other relevant passage in 2 Samuel makes clear, however, that Abiathar, not Ahimelech, is David's priest (2 Sam. 15:24, 29, 35; 17:15; 19:11). After David's death Abiathar is banished from Jerusalem because he backed the wrong son in the succession struggle. Abiathar backed Adonijah, the heir apparent. Zadok backed Solomon, the younger son of a questionable marriage. Solomon successfully usurped the throne, executed his brother Adonijah, and defrocked and banished Abiathar from Jerusalem (1 Kgs. 2:26–27). Solomon then "put the priest Zadok in the place of Abiathar" (1 Kgs. 2:35).

issue is thus settled. Nothing is made of their nonpriestly status. For Jesus, however, that is precisely why the story is significant. The physical hunger of David and his companions took precedence over purity concerns raised by the fact that they were not priests. The hospitality of God, symbolized in the table of the bread of the presence, is not limited by requirements of priestly purity. The Pharisees, though right to "democratize" the priesthood to include all Jews, were wrong to read sabbath through the lens of cultic and cultural purity. For Jesus, sabbath is properly interpreted through the hospitality code and the traditions of gleaning and sabbath year. The Pharisees see sabbath observance as a sign of cultural distinctiveness and cultic purity. Jesus sees sabbath as a sign of justice for the vulnerable poor. For Jesus, sabbath is a "little jubilee."

Jesus takes the exceptional case in 1 Samuel 21 and makes it the rule. David's feeding himself and his comrades in an emergency situation provides the fundamental principle by which sabbath is properly understood.

David is on the run from the paranoid King Saul. The reader knows—Saul only suspects—that God has withdrawn support from Saul and has secretly elected David king. Ahimelech pays with his life for the hospitality he has shown to David. David's eating the bread of the presence thus comes at a dangerous moment of historical transition, when the clashing sovereignties of past and future collide, with dangerous consequences for those who side with the new regime against the old.

The disputes between Jesus and his opponents in Mark take place in a comparable moment of transition. New wine requires new wineskins because the old will certainly burst. Sabbath is properly observed by the rules of the new age, the rules of radical hospitality implied in the table of the bread of presence and amplified by narrative echoes of gleaning and sabbath year. In the festive superabundance of God's in-breaking reign, keeping sabbath is above all a sign of God's boundless mercy and unlimited care. Matthew makes this point explicitly with Jesus' quoting Hosea 6:6 (cf. Isa. 1:12–17; Mic. 6:6–8): "If you had known what this means, 'I desire mercy and not sacrifice,' you would not have condemned the guiltless." In the era of new wineskins, the true significance of sabbath-keeping is clarified: "Sabbath is made for the human… the human being is lord even of the sabbath."

The scene now shifts to the synagogue. The principle of sabbath observance established in the field is brought inside the community of worship. There, Jesus encounters a man with a disabled hand. Throughout the Hebrew Scriptures, the hand symbolizes power, the ability to manipulate the world for a desired purpose. With a withered hand, this man is literally and figuratively disempowered, consigning him to a social-economic status like that adopted by Jesus' disciples when they gleaned from the grainfields on the sabbath—thus the connection of these two stories in the gospels.

Jesus' opponents watch him closely to see if he will heal on the sabbath, leaving himself vulnerable to prosecution for violating religious law. Their understanding of sabbath is inherently flawed.

Though it is conceivable that some ancient interpreters of Jewish law considered healing to be a violation of sabbath, this was not the view that became normative in Judaism. As Raphael Jospe observes,[5] the Talmudic norm that "saving life supersedes the sabbath" (*piquah nefesh doheh shabbat*) is deduced from Exodus 31:3 and Leviticus 18:5.

> From where [do we learn] that even a doubtful [case of saving] life supersedes the sabbath? Rabbi Abbahu said in the name of Rabbi Yohanan: "Nevertheless observe my sabbaths" [Exod. 31:3]… The Torah says: For his sake, desecrate the sabbath, so that he may sit and observe many sabbaths… They taught: He who hastens [to save a life by desecrating the sabbath] is praiseworthy; one who is asked is condemned; one who asks, sheds blood."[6] (Jerusalem Talmud, *Yoma* 8:5)

The Mishnah draws the principle from the last words of Leviticus 18:5, "by which he should live." "From where [do we learn] that saving a life supersedes the sabbath? Rabbi Judah said that Samuel said: As it is written, 'Observe my statutes and my ordinances which a person should do and by which he should live,' and not by which he should die" (*Yoma* 5:2). Jospe cites an extended comment from the

---

[5]The following references to Talmud and Talmudic commentaries are cited by Jospe, *Jubilee Challenge*, 82–83.

[6]Rabbi Israel Meir Ha-Kohen Kagan explains the curious statements about "the one who is asked" and "the one who asks" as follows: "That person who pretends to be pious and fears desecrating the sabbath for such a sick person…sheds blood, for while he goes to ask, the sick person may become even weaker and may be endangered…The local rabbi should have publicly taught the lesson, so that all the people might know, and would not need to ask him." Cited by Jospe, *Jubilee Challenge*, 83.

great twelfth-century interpreter of Jewish law Maimonides that bears repeating here:

> The sabbath and all the other commandments are superseded by danger to life…When there is doubt as to whether or not it is necessary to desecrate the sabbath…one desecrates the sabbath, for a dubious [case of saving a] life supersedes the sabbath. The general rule is: In the case of a sick person who is in danger, the sabbath is like a weekday for anything [the patient] may need. These things [in healing on the sabbath] should not be done by non-Jews or by minors or by slaves or by women, so that the sabbath should not become light in their view. [They should be done] by the leaders and the sages of Israel. It is forbidden to hesitate to desecrate the sabbath for a sick person who is in danger, as it says, "Which a person should do and by which he should live," and not by which he should die. Thus you learn that the ordinances of the Torah are not vengeful, but [bring] compassion and kindness and peace to the world.[7]

Jesus' opponents set up a false dispute, and in the process show that they fundamentally misunderstand the significance of sabbath. Jesus stands squarely within Jewish tradition by healing on the sabbath. By restoring the man's hand, Jesus restores his ability to work and, therefore, to rest from work on the seventh day. He has "violated" sabbath so the man may "observe many sabbaths." Saving a life supersedes the sabbath.

Several narrative features drive home the orthodoxy of Jesus' action. Jesus summons the man "to the center." His disability has put him at the social margins. His healing puts him back in the middle of things. Jesus poses the question of healing as the rabbis do, as an either/or issue of right and wrong: "Is it permissible to do good or evil on the sabbath?" Not to heal when you have the power to do so is to shed blood. Doing nothing is not a "third option"; it is the second, "evil" option. The choice is to do good (heal) or to do evil (refuse to heal). And on a sabbath that is made for the human, the only moral choice is to do good.

---

[7]Mishnah Torah, *Hilkhot Shabbat* 2:1–3.

Mark uses theologically loaded language to associate Jesus' opponents with the enemies of Israel. Jesus is grieved at "their hard-heartedness," an obvious allusion to the exodus story. The opponents who see the healing of the man as an opportunity to trap Jesus are playing the role of the hard-hearted pharaoh. Jesus' order to the man to "stretch out the hand" echoes the exodus story as well. Moses and Aaron "stretch out" the "hand" to invoke the miraculous plagues that ultimately free Israel from Egyptian bondage. At the sea, Yahweh's outstretched hand rescues Israel: "Your right hand, O Yahweh, glorious in power—your right hand, O Yahweh, shattered the enemy… You stretched out your right hand, the earth swallowed them…by the might of your arm, they became still as stone" (Exod. 15:6, 12, 16). By asking the man to "stretch out the hand," Jesus invites him to play the role of Moses and Aaron, to be the liberating instrument of God. Importantly, it is the man with the withered hand who does the work. Jesus commands. The man stretches out his own hand, and "the hand was restored." Participating in his own healing, the man becomes an instrument of God's liberation. The narrative allusions to the exodus story cast his healing as a symbol of the broader empowerment of disempowered Israel.

Plucking grain and healing the man with a withered hand are integrated parts of a narrative whole stitched together at the center by Jesus' definitive statement about sabbath-keeping: "The sabbath was made for the human, not the human for the sabbath. Therefore, the human being is lord even of the sabbath." Echoes of the gleaning and hospitality codes and unmistakable allusions to the exodus tradition associate sabbath with liberation and social justice. As with sabbath and sabbath-year laws bound together in Exodus 23:9–12 by concern for the life of the marginal resident alien, Jesus' actions and teaching on the sabbath interpret the seventh day through the imperatives of social justice, especially material care for the most vulnerable. Sabbath is a "little sabbath year," a "little jubilee," a weekly celebration of God's healing care and the grand gestures of social reform that sometimes set things right. Sabbath is properly understood and practiced with a lavishly generous spirit appropriate to this superabundant era of new wineskins, in which the sick are healed, sinners are forgiven, and the morally and culturally impure are invited to the center and restored.

A Woman Bent Double

Now it happened that he was teaching in one of the synagogues on the sabbath. Suddenly, there was a woman who had had a weakening spirit for eighteen years. She was bent over and not able to stand erect at all. Seeing her, Jesus called out to her and said, "Woman, you are set free from your weakness!" He laid hands on her, and she immediately straightened up and began praising God. But the president of the synagogue, angry that Jesus had healed on the sabbath, said to the crowd, "There are six days to do work. So come to be healed on those days, not on the sabbath day!" But the Lord answered him and said, "Hypocrites! Doesn't each one of you on the sabbath release his ox and donkey from the manger and lead it away to give it water? Shouldn't this daughter of Abraham, whom Satan has bound for eighteen years, be released from this bondage on the sabbath day?" When he said this, all his opponents were dishonored, and the whole crowd rejoiced at all the noteworthy things he was doing. (Luke 13:10–17)

This story is unique to Luke, but the issue at dispute is the same as that in the story of the man with a withered hand. The leader of the synagogue where the healing takes place criticizes Jesus for healing on the sabbath day. Jesus' response puts all his opponents to shame—the worst possible result for them in this culture of honor and shame.

Jesus' retort connects sabbath observance with the humanitarian rationale for sabbath in the primary sabbath laws (Exod. 20:10; 23:12; Deut. 5:14) and for release in the sabbath-year traditions (Exod. 23:11; Deut. 15:1–3). The connection centers on the imagery of "binding" and "releasing" the ox and donkey.

Under the principle of "saving a life" (*piquah nefesh*) discussed previously, it is permitted to do work on sabbath that provides necessary sustenance to farm animals or relieves their suffering. The purpose of sabbath is "that your ox and your donkey may have relief" (Exod. 23:12). Animals must be fed and cows must be milked, though there can be no financial benefit to the household from the milk taken on sabbath.[8]

---

[8] Jospe, *Jubilee Challenge*, 84.

But the image of untying and releasing the ox and donkey also connects the story of the woman's healing with sabbath-year release. As we saw in chapter 5 in the discussion of "shaking off the yoke" of debt in Nehemiah 5:13,[9] indebtedness, servitude, and oppression are often described as bearing a yoke. The root meaning of *shemittah* in the sabbath-year passages refers to loosening a yoke and letting it drop from the shoulders. With shoulders now unbound, the one released can stand completely erect.

By the very nature of her debilitating ailment, the woman is a living embodiment of the standard metaphor for indebtedness and oppression. She is "bent over," as if bearing a yoke. Her physical condition cries out for release. Jesus reminds his opponents that they release their yoked animals on sabbath and, by his rhetorical question, urges sabbath release for the similarly yoked and bound daughter of Abraham. The opponents are shamed by his words because they have fundamentally misunderstood the nature and purpose of sabbath. Sabbath at its very heart is a day of release. The woman bent over embodied debt and oppression. The woman, now able to stand erect, embodies the essence of sabbath as sabbath-year release. As in the other sabbath controversy stories, sabbath in this story is properly understood and observed as a celebration of abundant life, healing, and sabbath-year justice.

A Man with Dropsy

It happened that he went to the house of someone who was a leader of the Pharisees on sabbath to eat bread. And they were watching him closely. Suddenly, a man who had dropsy was right in front of him. Jesus responded by saying to the lawyers and Pharisees, "Is it permissible to heal on the sabbath or not?" They were silent. Then, taking hold of him, he cured and released him. Then he said to them, "Which of you, when a donkey or ox falls into a cistern, won't immediately pull it out on the sabbath day?" And they were unable to reply to this. (Luke 14:1–6)

The story of healing the man with dropsy is patterned closely after the story of the man with a withered hand. Jesus' opponents "were

---

[9]For bibliography on debt, taxes, and slavery as a "burden" or "yoke" in ancient Near Eastern literature, see Weinfeld, *Social Justice*, 84, n. 38, and 171, n. 69.

watching him closely" (v. 1; cf. 6:7; Mark 3:2). He asks them what is permissible under the law, though his question is more direct this time: "Is it permissible to heal on the sabbath, or not?" (v. 3; cf. 6:9; Mark 3:4). But his opponents "were silent" (v. 4; cf. Mark 3:4).

The interpretive key to this sabbath controversy story comes in verses 4–5, in Jesus' action toward the man and his rhetorical question that explains why he heals on sabbath. The rhetorical question associates sabbath with the rationale for sabbath in Exodus 23:12 and the Decalogue (Exod. 20:10, Deut. 5:14). "Which of you, when a donkey or ox falls into a cistern, won't immediately pull it out on the sabbath day?" The ancient manuscripts are divided on whether to read "donkey" (*onos*) or "son" (*huios*) in this verse. The words are very close in Greek, and one can easily imagine a scribal error substituting one word for the other. In light of the explicit mention of "donkey" and "ox" in the sabbath law in Exodus 23:12 (cf. 23:4; Deut. 22:4), it seems more likely that "donkey or ox" is the original reading in Luke. A later scribe, who perhaps missed the allusion to the sabbath law, may have inadvertently or deliberately altered the first two letters of *onos* to read "son" rather than "donkey." The description of the situation—an animal falling "into a cistern"—is probably a verbal play on the man's disease, severe fluid retention. But the fact that the animal is a "donkey" or "ox," a beast of burden—as opposed to a sheep or goat, for example—rhetorically associates healing in this story with the release tradition already linked with healing in the case of the woman bent over.

The connection with sabbath-year release is sealed in the description of the act of healing itself: "Taking hold of him, he cured and released him." Though often translated "let him go" (RSV) or "sent him away" (NRSV), the verb I have translated "released" (*apelusen*) is from the same root (*luo*) as the word translated "release" or "untie" in the story of the woman bent double. Jesus healed the man and thus "released" him. Healing is not only permissible on the sabbath, it is the very essence of sabbath, properly interpreted—as Luke suggests by the words he chooses—through the lens of sabbath-year and jubilee release.

Spiritual Blindness

The core issues at stake in John 9:1–41 are the identity of Jesus as Messiah and the proper response to him. Blindness and sight function

metaphorically to describe the ability of Jesus' contemporaries to per-
ceive his true nature as the one sent from God. Healing is a metaphor
for belief in Jesus as Son of God. Sabbath is peripheral to the central
point of the narrative. It appears as an afterthought, a parenthetical
aside (v. 14). Its narrative function is to set up and highlight the spiritual blindness of "some of the Pharisees," who fail to see what is perfectly obvious to a blind man: that Jesus is the Son of God. Having
completed its narrative task in verse 16, sabbath disappears as an issue
in the story.

Sabbath and Abundant Life

Sharon Ringe's excellent and accessible monograph *Jesus, Liberation, and the Biblical Jubilee*[10] covers major sabbath-year and jubilee
references in the gospels. I will not repeat or try to improve upon her
very fine analysis of texts, but I do have brief comments about three
blocks of Jesus material that highlight sabbath-as-jubilee themes.

Jesus' Mission: Release to Captives

> When he entered Nazareth where he was raised, he went, as
> was his custom on the sabbath day, into the synagogue. And
> he stood up to read. The scroll of the prophet Isaiah was
> given to him. He unrolled the scroll, finding the place where
> it is written, "The spirit of the Lord is upon me, because he
> has anointed me to bring good news to the poor, he has sent
> me to announce release [*aphesin*] to captives and recovery of
> sight to the blind, to send out the shattered in release [*aphesei*],
> to announce the acceptable year of the Lord." Then he rolled
> up the scroll, gave it to the attendant, and sat down. The eyes
> of everyone in the synagogue were fixed on him. Then he
> began to say to them, "Today, this writing has been fulfilled
> in your hearing!" (Luke 4:16–21)

Sabbath provides the setting for Jesus' inaugural sermon in Luke 4.
Jesus has just returned from his Moses-like forty-day temptation in
the wilderness, following his baptism. Having survived the initiation
ordeal, he returns to his home region, Galilee, "filled with the power

---

[10]Sharon H. Ringe, *Jesus, Liberation, and the Biblical Jubilee: Images for Ethics and
Christology,* Overtures to Biblical Theology (Philadelphia: Fortress, 1985).

of the Spirit" (4:14). Word about him spread throughout the region, and he began to teach in their synagogues. But the narrative kickoff for his preaching career, according to Luke, comes when he returns to Nazareth, the place where he was raised. "He went, as was his custom on the sabbath day, into the synagogue. And he stood up to read" (v. 16).

Handed the Isaiah scroll, Jesus searches for the *derôr* (liberty) passage in Isaiah 61. Reading the prophet's announcement of call, Jesus assumes the role of the one anointed by God to bring good news to the poor. But his interpretation of the passage and the crowd's response dramatically shift the prophetic impact of the words. In the social-political context of Third Isaiah at the end of Babylonian exile, the prophecy offers hope for Israel's restoration after years of oppression by a foreign empire. The poor, the captives, the shattered oppressed are the prisoners of Babylonian exile, whose eyes have adjusted to the dank darkness of their political dungeon and now open to the bright sun of freedom. Third Isaiah offers good news to oppressed Israel set at liberty in this year of Yahweh's favor, when mighty Babylon falls and its captives are released. The Nazarene congregation understands the significance of the Isaiah passage for their own subservience to Rome. The people are elated at Jesus' militant proclamation: "Today, this writing has been fulfilled in your hearing!"

But Jesus, oblivious to the well-tested preacher's wisdom that "less is more," that you should know when to sit down, and to quit while you're ahead, continues with a sermon that makes the congregation want to kill him. Citing the healing stories "Elijah and the widow of Zarephath" (1 Kgs. 17:1–16) and "Elisha and Naaman of Syria" (2 Kgs. 5:1–14), Jesus flips the Third Isaiah passage on its head, arguing that in times of crisis such as these, Yahweh sends prophets to rescue non-Israelites. Contrary to the expectations of the Nazarene congregation, good news to the poor is good news to Gentiles!

This astonishing reversal no doubt made sense to Luke's mixed Jewish and Gentile Christian audience, since his entire two-volume history, Luke-Acts, is geared toward the "Gentile mission," the early church's phenomenal outreach to non-Jewish populations. The good news that turns sour for Jesus' Nazarene audience becomes very good news for the implied audience of Luke's narrative, Gentile Christians and Jewish-Christian advocates of the Gentile mission. But Jesus' word offers a challenge to the church as well. The jubilee reversal envisioned in the Isaiah passage and in Jesus' surprising interpretation offers a word of hope to everyone who stands on the outside of the community. Though it supports the beliefs of Luke's Christian community, the prophetic power of the story resists domestication. It offers a word of warning to all who think of themselves as God's elect—even Luke's own Gentile Christian community. Jesus' sabbath-day sermon in Nazareth urges humility and gratitude and promises a surprising superabundance of grace in this moment of crisis and jubilee hope.

Jesus' Prayer: Release our Debts!

You should pray in this manner: "Our father in heaven, holy is your name. Let your kingdom come! Let your will be done—as in heaven, so on earth! Give us today our bread for tomorrow. Release us from our debts, as we also release our debtors. Do not lead us into trial, but save us from evil." For if you release others from their false steps, your father in heaven will also release you. But if you do not release others, your father in heaven will not release your false steps. (Matt. 6:9–15)

He said to them, "Whenever you pray, say, 'Father, holy is your name. Let your kingdom come! Give us each day our bread for tomorrow. And release us from our sins, for we also release everyone who is indebted to us. And do not lead us into trial." (Luke 11:2–4)

Both versions of the Lord's Prayer[11] make allusions to sabbath-year release and the sabbath-manna story. The petition in Matthew "release us from our debts as we also release our debtors" connects with the biblical *shemittah* tradition by the rhetoric of "debt" (*opheilema*) and "release" (*aphiemi*). Luke uses the somewhat different term "sins" (*hamartias*) in the first half of the petition, but uses "debtors" (*opheilonti*) in the second half. Both use the verb *aphes*, often translated "forgive," which I translate "release." The semantic range of the root verb *aphiemi* ("to loose, release, or set free") is virtually identical with that of the Hebrew verb *shamat* ("to loose or release") in the seventh-year laws in Deuteronomy 15 and Exodus 23.

---

[11] Mark has a very brief statement on prayer that may have inspired the more lengthy elaboration in the Lord's Prayer in Matthew and Luke. "And whenever you stand to pray, if you have something against someone, release it, so that your father in heaven will also release you from your false steps" (Mark 11:25).

In fact, this is precisely the Greek word that the Septuagint uses to translate *shamat* and *shemittah* in Deuteronomy 15:1–3 and Exodus 23:11. While "forgiving debt," in the context of the Lord's Prayer, may well mean more than the economic release envisioned in the Hebrew Scriptures, it certainly does not mean anything less than economic liberation.

The economic dimension of the Lord's Prayer is also reflected in the difficult-to-translate petition for bread (Matt 6:11; Luke 11:3). The confusion centers on the curious term *epiousios*, "that which is necessary for each day" ("daily") or "that which is necessary for the following day" ("tomorrow's"). Either way, the biblical allusion is clear. By "daily" or "tomorrow's" bread, Jesus refers to the sabbath-manna story in Exodus 16, where "some gathered more, some gathered less, but when they measured it with an omer, the ones with more had no surplus and the ones with less had no shortage" (Exod. 16:18). "Daily" or "tomorrow's" bread is the miraculous manna of sabbath utopia. Translating *epiousios* as "tomorrow's" bread makes the explicit connection with the double portion of manna (Exod. 16:22) that appears on the sixth day so that Israel can observe sabbath on the seventh day. "Tomorrow's bread" is the gracious abundance God wills for all people, especially those who are economically vulnerable.

Structuring his model prayer on sabbath-manna and debt release, Jesus defines the coming "kingdom" of God as an era of economic freedom and social solidarity in which all people have what they need to survive. And he summons his disciples to a prayerful spirituality shaped in the contours of sabbath and sabbath-year justice.

The Fatal Greed of a Rich Fool

> Then he told them a parable: The land of a certain rich man produced abundantly. And he thought to himself, "What should I do, since I do not have a place to store my crops?" He said, "This is what I will do! I will pull down my barns and build bigger ones. And I will store all of my wheat and my goods there! And I will say to my soul, 'Soul, you have put away many goods for many years! Relax! Eat, drink, be merry!'" But God said to him, "Fool! Tonight, your soul is required of you!" So it goes with those who put away things for themselves, but are not rich toward God. (Luke 12:16–21)

Bernard Brandon Scott appropriately titles this story "How To Mismanage a Miracle."[12] The Joseph tradition (Genesis 41) looms large over the parable. The rich man's astounding bounty prompts him to pull down his barns and build bigger ones, as Joseph did for Egypt in Genesis 41:33–36. But Joseph stored the surplus of seven good years as "a reserve for the land…so that the land may not perish because of the famine" that would follow in the seven lean years (v. 36). The rich man in Jesus' parable, by contrast, plans to build bigger barns for his own private pleasure, so he can "eat, drink, and be merry."

The Joseph story reflects the widely held belief in the ancient world that goods exist in limited supply.[13] Excessive accumulation by one means shortage for others. The economy of limited goods also means that an excessive harvest one year may be a sign of reduced harvest in years to come—a reality that is obvious to Joseph and utterly lost on the rich man in Jesus' parable. This idea underlies the double portion of manna on the sixth day in the sabbath-manna story (Exod. 16:29) and the triple harvest in the sixth year before sabbath year and jubilee (Lev. 25:20–22). The double portion on the sixth day is preparation for seventh-day sabbath, when there will be no manna to gather. The triple harvest in the sixth year provides enough to eat in the seventh year, when there will be no agriculture at all, and in the eighth year until the crops mature.

The rich man in Jesus' parable is a "fool" because he fundamentally misunderstands the purpose of the miraculous harvest. His extraordinary good fortune is a sign of sabbath, sabbath year, and jubilee—a sixth-day double bounty to make sabbath self-restraint possible, a sixth-year triple harvest before sabbath year and jubilee are proclaimed. The rich man foolishly assumes that his good fortune should be spent on his own private enjoyment rather than used for the good of the community. He thus fails the sabbath test set up by God in Exodus 16:4. Planning to hoard the miraculous provision of food rather than sharing it for the common good, he allows his miraculous bounty to spoil and breed worms. His doubts about tomorrow and God's ongoing provision of enough to survive lead to fear.

---

[12]Bernard Brandon Scott, *Hear Then the Parable* (Minneapolis: Fortress, 1989), 129–49.

[13]Malina, *New Testament World*, 90–116.

And fear leads to greed, a foolish attempt to control tomorrow by hoarding today. But controlling his world proves futile. Tonight his soul is required of him. Failing to trust that God will provide enough for him and his community to survive, the rich man hoards limited goods, denies others the ability to survive the coming shortage, and thus condemns his own soul.

Scott argues that the rich man in this story has committed idolatry, usurping the harvest that God intended for the long-term welfare of the community, but also usurping the story itself, replacing God's voice with his own:[14] "Soul, you have put away many goods for many years!" Greed is a secondary problem in this story. The fundamental issue is the proper attitude toward God as giver of life and prosperity. This is a parable about arrogance and idolatry, the foolish delusion that life is entirely the product of one's own hand.

The verses that follow the parable cast the issue of idolatrous arrogance in an even more piercing light. Verses 22–34 (cf. Matt 6) contain a series of sayings about wealth and anxiety. "Do not worry about your life, what you will eat or drink" (v. 22); "consider the ravens: they neither sow nor reap, they have neither storehouses nor barns, and yet God feeds them" (v. 24); "consider the lilies: they do not toil or spin, but, I tell you, even Solomon in all his glory was not clothed like one of them" (v. 27). These sayings speak of trust, faith in God to provide enough. The practical result of such confidence is unambiguous: "Do not be afraid, little flock...Sell your possessions and give alms" (vv. 32–33). The confidence to relinquish and redistribute wealth grows out of the assurance that God provides enough for abundant life for all.

In the broader context of this series of teachings on wealth, the rich fool's mortal sin is clarified as a failure to trust God. A miraculous harvest faithfully received is an occasion for sharing, a response that gratefully acknowledges God as gracious and able giver of bounty, today and tomorrow too. Generosity flows from trust. Selfishness grows from fear. Fear breeds obsession with survival, a craving for control. And obsessive craving is the stuff idols are made of.

The rich man's failure of nerve, his lack of faith, leads him to squander a sabbath and jubilee miracle and, in the process, to squander his own life.

---

[14]Scott, *Hear Then the Parable*, 134–39.

Summary

Through controversy stories about healing on sabbath, the gospels associate sabbath-keeping with hospitality codes, sabbath year, and jubilee. Sabbath is a sign of economic justice and social solidarity. Sabbath observance is a celebration of the new era of God's superabundant grace, especially toward those on the margins. Sabbath is a "little jubilee," the sign of a new era, the "kingdom of God," characterized by healing and radical hospitality for the outcast.

Healing on the sabbath, though presented as a major point of contention between Jesus and his opponents, is not a problem in orthodox Jewish interpretation. Talmud and interpreters of Talmud are unanimous in affirming the principle that "saving a life supersedes the sabbath." Jesus stands firmly within orthodox Jewish tradition when he heals on the sabbath.

The Lord's Prayer and the parable of the rich fool connect sabbath with sabbath-year release and sabbath-manna to advocate a Christian spirituality built on economic justice and social solidarity. Fundamentally misunderstanding the nature of his miraculous bounty, the rich fool fails to trust that God will continue to provide necessary sustenance. His fear breeds greed, which causes him to hoard what is graciously given for the common good.

9

A MODERN SPIRITUALITY OF SABBATH AND JUBILEE

Biblical sabbath, sabbath-year, and jubilee traditions spoke to very different social, economic, and political conditions than those we face today. In ancient Israel, the extended household was all-important. Concern for its long-term survival stood at the heart of social ethics and personal identity. But the economic demands of monarchy, especially its tax and compulsory labor requirements, undermined the economic viability and stability of households. An interest-lending system provided short-term help to households in crisis, but often accelerated their demise and consolidated wealth in the hands of a privileged few.

Nevertheless, kings took pride in their roles as householders of the nation and protectors of the weak. In Israel, Yahweh was celebrated as the divine sovereign who is "father" and "mother" of the people, provider of bounty, and champion of the vulnerable. Sabbath, sabbath year, and jubilee are grounded in the sovereign power and compassion of God.

145

Biblical sabbath-year and jubilee traditions have deep roots in ancient Near Eastern legal codes and royal decrees that sought to limit the devastating impact of debt and debt slavery on households. But as far as we know, Israel is the only ancient culture that attempted to institutionalize these social reforms as a regularly recurring event. Sabbath year is, in fact, a variety of reforms, focused on improving the lot of the poor. Jubilee is fairly late and largely utopian, but it provides some of the most important and revolutionary social-theological principles in the Bible. Sabbath-year and jubilee traditions are associated with Israel's sacred narrative of liberation from Egyptian slavery. They reflect the distinctive character of Yahweh and identity of Israel as Yahweh's people.

Sabbath traditions continue the social-economic focus of sabbath year. The sabbath day functions as a "little jubilee," a weekly celebration of the principles expressed in sabbath-year and jubilee release. The basic sabbath narratives celebrate a world of abundance, self-restraint, and social solidarity that reverses the everyday conditions of life under royal political economy. The world of creation-sabbath and sabbath-manna is a world of lavish abundance where everyone works who is able, everyone rests when her or his body requires rest, and every household has what it needs to survive.

Sabbath has a radically humanitarian rationale, centered on justice and relief for the most vulnerable members of the household, including beasts of burden. The prophets and histories expand the household ethic of sabbath-keeping to the nation as a whole. Proper sabbath observance requires active concern for the welfare of the poor. Sabbath reflects the character of Yahweh as hospitable host of Israel, a role symbolized in the sanctuary by the table of the bread of presence. Later passages, such as Isaiah 56, portray God's hospitality as universally expansive, embracing all the nations, including foreigners and the ritually impure.

The universal hospitality, lavish abundance, and social solidarity of sabbath year and jubilee shape Jesus' teaching about sabbath, illustrated in controversy stories. Jesus does not abolish sabbath-keeping, but takes the orthodox Jewish position that sabbath is observed for the benefit of people. By example, he teaches that sabbath is kept in acts of healing generosity and welcome for the outcast.

Sovereign God, Worthy Human

A theology and practice of sabbath in the modern world begins with the royal nature of God and human beings, created in God's image.

The monarchical metaphor is a problem for modern democratic societies that put less or no stock in the political authority of kings and queens. Indeed, the hierarchies of power symbolized in the metaphors of monarchy have proved destructive to democratic life and have been used to dampen the aspirations of oppressed peoples worldwide. Authorizing human beings to "rule the earth and subdue it" has certainly had disastrous consequences for the natural environment in the industrial age—though it is not at all clear that a gentler metaphor would have halted the march of industrial devastation in the modern period. There is ample reason to reject the monarchist metaphor and replace it with an image more democratic, egalitarian, humble, and kind to the life-supporting natural environment.

But the royal metaphor holds promise, as well. Portraying all human beings as queens and kings who bear the image of God is a powerful way to promote universal human rights, to resist violence and repression, and to build a more democratic and just world. Genesis 1, though built conceptually on the model of monarchy, is amazingly egalitarian. Men and women share the power of governance without distinction of rank or degree—a striking depiction for its time and culture. If "every man is a king," as American politician Huey Long used to say, and "every woman is a queen," as Genesis 1 would add, then no one should live like a slave, submitting "graciously" or otherwise to the power of another.

Even the rhetoric of redemption can be redeemed. By buying the ownership rights to Israel, Yahweh effectively takes its people off the slave market. As "slaves of God" they can serve no human master. As instrument of blessing to all the nations of the earth, Israel conveys the blessing of freedom to everyone else as well. Social, economic, political, and cultural bondage, though often justified as "natural order" and "divine will," are in fact arrogant attempts to commandeer the rightful power of God. Oppression is idolatry! In the fitting slogan of American Revolutionary Christians, "No king but King Jesus!" Redeemed by God, all people are by nature free!

The rhetoric of God's sovereignty in the world also counters modern ideologies of self-sufficiency and personal control. The advance of technology in the twentieth century has made life better. But for all our ability to manipulate the world, we still operate within ultimately fatal limits. We still die. We still fall victim to freak accidents, random acts of violence, and untreatable disease. Our fundamental inability to control important aspects of our lives seems all the more cruel in the face of our mind-boggling ability to control so much of what happens to us. The sovereignty of God in the world is a useful reminder in the modern age that we do not control everything. We govern some things and are responsible for the way we exercise authority in the world. But many of life's important things are out of our hands.

Sovereignty in the world belongs to us as kings and queens in the image of God, but it is given to us as a sacred trust. Our power to control is not absolute. Our sovereign authority is by its very nature shared. Power hoarded fouls and evaporates. Power shared grows and blesses the world. The royal authority of women and men has a divine model. The God who lavishly provides and joyfully celebrates creation's every detail authorizes humans to rule in the earth with joy, awe, and respectful delight.

Household Justice

In the Bible, the social ethics of sabbath and jubilee are rooted in ethics of household and clan solidarity. Social responsibility begins in the home and extends outward. A modern spirituality of sabbath and jubilee begins with justice in the household, with solidarity and shared power. Justice and peace in communities and nations are built on caring and respectful relationships in families, between partners and between parents and children. People who are valued at home are much more likely to value others. Households are classrooms in human interaction. Homes shaped by a spirituality of sabbath and jubilee offer daily instruction in being the image of God and honoring that image in every other person.

Households in ancient Israel were structured very differently than households in many places today. But sabbath and jubilee principles of abundance and self-restraint continue to offer a useful and liberating word. Globalizing economy and ever more sophisticated technologies offer great potential for stronger families and better lives.

But we must figure out boundaries, set limits to the ubiquitous work-place, find ways to deliver sufficient and timely relief for families, communities, and ecosystems pressured by the sometimes brutal logic of markets. Practical solutions to these problems will necessarily shift and change over time. But the values of abundance, celebration, and social solidarity that lie at the heart of biblical sabbath and jubilee offer enduring principles by which to shape our lives together, first in families and also in communities, nations, and the world.

We are often urged to think globally and act locally. The house-hold ethic at the heart of sabbath and jubilee calls us also to think locally when we act globally, to build a just world from the family up.

Economics and Ecology of Sabbath and Jubilee

Sabbath and jubilee in Bible times were a mixture of utopian and hard-but-practical programs of action. In the modern world, the spe-cifics of biblical sabbath and jubilee are moot or impossible. But the principles of social solidarity, abundance and self-restraint, and con-cern for the long-term survival of families can be adapted and applied.

A modern economics of sabbath and jubilee must hold utopian ideals in tension with what can actually be achieved. The point of sabbath and jubilee justice is neither pie-in-the-sky by-and-by nor human sacrifice on the altar of "practical politics." Sabbath and jubi-lee consciousness does not accept the "intractability" of poverty and violence. But neither does it countenance principled paralysis over our failure to achieve utopia. It will push for the dignity and well-being of every single person, but it must never allow the perfect to become the enemy of the possible.

To the impoverished and violated, sabbath and jubilee offer hope and issue a call to action. God wills that everyone have enough to survive and flourish. Homelessness, starvation, violence, and degrad-ing labor are not "the way of the world," immutable laws of the uni-verse that cannot be overturned. Poverty and degradation are unnatural in the sabbath and jubilee view. Sustaining abundant life for all is the fundamental logic of creation, the vocation of every human being. All people have the right to sufficient food, clothing, housing, safety, and dignity. The struggle for justice has divine sanction.

To the comfortable, sabbath and jubilee offer assurance and call for self-examination. The assurance is that God desires not the im-poverishment of the rich, but the enrichment of the poor. Wealth is neither an embarrassment nor a spiritual danger if it is shared with the same generosity as that shown by God through the lavishly productive world. Faithful confidence in God frees us to share boldly. We are also called to honestly evaluate personal patterns of consumption and giving and to see our place in larger systems of production and distribution. Sabbath and jubilee promise abundance, but call for self-restraint and generous sharing.

Nowhere is the need for sabbath and jubilee greater than in efforts to relieve the crushing burden of debt on poor nations. Though not a simple matter to resolve, the international debt burden carried by the poorest nations, primarily in war-torn and poverty-stricken regions of Africa and Latin America, cries out for dramatic institutional solutions akin to biblical *shemittah* (release) and *derôr* (liberty).

"Debt restructuring" programs imposed on these countries by the International Monetary Fund and other lenders have had devastating social and environmental consequences. Poor countries have cut wages and slashed health care and education programs to attract international investment and the "hard currency" they need to keep paying on their debt. In many cases, the amount of the original loan has been repaid. They are paying interest on the interest and will never be able to pay off the debt. Tanzania spends nine times more on debt repayments than on health care.[1] Mozambique spends 33 percent of its national budget on debt payments, 3 percent on health, and 8 percent on education.[2] Every child born in Nicaragua inherits more than $2000 of debt at birth, though the average annual income there is $390.[3] The United Nations estimates that if funds currently paid out on debt in these severely indebted nations were diverted back into health care and education, the lives of seven million children could be saved within a year.[4]

Many of the loans, made in the context of the Cold War, were given to dictatorial governments that squandered the principal on graft, environmentally destructive and economically unviable projects, and military police. A considerable portion was used to subsidize investment by Western companies. Children and working families in

---

[1]Source: Oxfam.

[2]Source: Jubilee 2000/Jubilee 2000 Coalition, 1 Rivington Street, London EC2A 3DT, www.jubilee2000uk.org; cf. *Jubilee Justice: The Times Call Us* (Pax Christi USA), 61.

[3]Source: Jubilee 2000/USA Jubilee 2000/USA, 222 East Capitol Street, NE, Washington, DC 20003-1036, www.j2000usa.org.

[4]Source: Jubilee 2000/UK.

these countries today are repaying loans that financed the repression and impoverishment of their own families. It is a modern twist on the ancient abomination of "boiling the kid in the mother's milk" (Exod. 23:19; 34:26; Deut. 14:21).

Since only about 10 percent of these nations' debt is owed to private banks,[5] the lion's share could be reduced or canceled by direct government action of lending nations. Debt release for poor countries is practical, if the political will can be mustered. The sabbath and jubilee vision of abundant life for all and its conviction that debt burdens have limits may help change the moral climate and create the necessary political environment for substantial debt relief.

Ecological Justice in a Sabbath and Jubilee World

In the biblical traditions of sabbath and jubilee, the earth has its own vocation and purpose. Earth is called to flourishing life, to provide a hospitable, luxurious home for all earth's creatures, especially human beings. When our own inattentive, greedy, or excessive lifestyles damage the earth's ability to provide a comfortable home for human life, we undermine earth's vocation of worship and generous hospitality.

Justice for the earth begins with daily choices of individuals and households, but more importantly it depends on the rules and structures of social-economic life. Assumptions of scarcity and unlimited needs and wants are the twin pillars of classical economic theory. These assumptions underlie actual economic decisions made by firms and governments, creating an imperative toward unlimited economic growth. Under these assumptions, the only humane response to poverty and unemployment is constantly to expand the economic pie, creating more wealth and cutting more people in for a slice. The social and ecological problems created by unlimited economic growth are, in this view, the unavoidable costs of bringing the necessities of life to greater numbers of people. Sabbath and jubilee principles of abundance and self-restraint run counter to these largely unquestioned assumptions of contemporary economics, and focus attention on better distribution, rather than greater levels of production. The problem is not scarcity, but the will to share. The solution is lavish generosity and faithful confidence in God's abundant care.

---

[5]About half of the debt is owed directly to individual governments—Japan, the United States, Britain, Canada, France, Germany, and Italy. About 40 percent is owed to the World Bank and International Monetary Fund, which essentially are run by the same governments. Source: Jubilee 2000/UK.

Above all, a sabbath and jubilee consciousness perceives the world as the blessed gift of God. Commodities are bought and sold, traded and trashed. Gifts, however, communicate the giver. They express the personality and love of the one who gives them. They are treated rightly, therefore, with utmost honor and care. Through sabbath and jubilee eyes, creation is seen as the blessed gift of God, the cherished, constant reminder of the God who wills abundant life for all.

A Spirituality of Sabbath and Jubilee

In the world of sabbath and jubilee, the personal is the political. These traditions root the call to justice in an abiding sense of God's gracious care and in personal and household disciplines of gratitude and respect. These orientations toward life are grounded in the fundamental worth of ourselves and of all human beings, created male and female, diverse but equal, in the image of God. Actions of justice are prayers of gratitude for abundant life lavishly given. And spiritual disciplines of contemplation and praise are ongoing celebrations of the just world that God wills and that we are called to build.

Scripture Index[1]

GENESIS

1	23, 59, 61–63, 73, 75, 96–97, 99, 101–2
1:1—2:4a	63, 79–94
1:1	83, 87
1:1–2	88
1:2—2:3	87–88
1:2	82–83, 90
1:3	84, 89–90
1:5	89
1:6–10	83
1:6–9	89
1:13	89
1:14–17	84
1:14	89
1:19	89
1:20	84, 89
1:22	90, 92
1:23–24	89
1:26–28	61, 91, 107
1:28	73, 90–92
1:29–30	73
1:31	87
2:1–4	88
2:1	87
2:3	92–93
2:4	87
2:24	8
4:10	50
12:2	90
12:3	20
14	27
14:13	28
14:14	28
14:17–24	28
14:20	29
17:20	90
18:1–15	117
18:21	50
19:13	50
22:17	90
24:28	8
25:29–34	11
26:3–4	90
26:24	90
27:28	85
27:40	49
28:18–22	85
31:1–2	34
31:7	34
31:13	85
31:38	34
31:41–42	34
35:1–15	85
39:17	26
37:1—50:26	27
39:14	27
39:17	27
40:15	27
41:2–7	85
41:2–20	86
41:15	27
41:18–20	85
41:33–36	141
43:32	27

EXODUS

1:15–16	29
1:19	29
2:6–7	29
2:11–13	29
3:7	50
3:9	50, 52
3:10–15	33
3:18	29
3:20	33
3:21–22	33–34
4:4	33
4:13	33
4:21–23	33

[1]Where Hebrew and English versification differ, the English is noted in brackets.

4:28	33	16:4	141
5:1–2	33	16:17–18	100
5:3	29	16:18	140
5:22	33	16:19–30	99
6:1	33	16:22	140
6:6	62	16:29	141
6:10	33	16:31–35	100
7:2	33	19—20	71, 77
7:13–22	33	19:15	93
7:26–27 [8:1–2]	33	19:16	71
8:1–28 [5–32]	33	19:19	71
9:1–35	33	20:1–5	73
10:1–7	33	20:8–11	73, 105–9,
10:10	33		113
10:20–22	33	20:10	107, 134,
10:27	33		136
11:1	33	20:11	108
11:6	50	20:18	71
11:10	33	20:22—23:33	24, 51
12:30	50	21	5, 25–26,
12:33	33		32, 35,
12:35–36	33–34		44–45, 51,
13:15–17	33		68
14:4	33, 98	21:2–11	24–30, 32
14:5–8	33	21:2	24–25, 27,
14:16–17	33		29–30, 32,
14:21	33		47
14:26–27	33	21:3–4	25
14:27	49	21:5–6	25, 32
14:31	98	21:7–11	25–26
15	96–97	21:17	9
15:1–18	97–98	21:26–27	24
15:6	133	22:15–16 [16–17]	26
15:7	33	22:20–26 [21–27]	50
15:12	133	22:20–23 [21–24]	13
15:13	62	22:20[21]	52
15:14–16	98	22:21 [22]	13
15:16	133	22:24 [25]	12
15:17–18	98	22:25–26 [26–27]	13
15:22–27	98	23	5, 23, 37,
16	23, 59,		59, 61, 63,
	62–63,		65, 77, 139
	96–97, 99,	23:4	136
	101–2	23:9–12	24, 51–55,
16:2–33	94–101		106,
16:4–5	99		127–28, 133

23:10–11	13, 23, 51, 53–54, 56, 113	25:1	72
		25:2–7	54
		25:4	23
23:11	134, 140	25:5–7	59–60
23:12	24, 61, 113, 134, 136	25:8–55	65–72
		25:8–13	65
23:15	34	25:9	71
23:19	151	25:10	45, 66–68
23:27–28	33	25:11–12	60
25:23–30	116	25:18–24	23, 54
26:35	116	25:19–22	102
30:22–38	85	25:20–24	58–62
31:3	131	25:20–22	60, 141
31:14	107	25:23	61
33:2	33	25:25	18
33:18–23	111	25:25–34	70
34:20	34	25:35–55	67
34:21	107, 128	25:35–43	70
34:26	151	25:35–37	12
35:2–3	107	25:35	68
35:13	116	25:36–37	47, 70
39:3	84	25:39–42	70
40:22–23	116	25:39	45, 67
		25:41	68
LEVITICUS		25:42	30, 45, 61–62
1:1	58		
7:36	85	25:47–55	70
7:38	58	25:55	30, 45, 70
8:10–13	85	26	57, 73, 75
12:2–5	93	26:1–13	72–74
15:18	93	26:2	115
16:1–34	71	26:9	73
18:5	131	26:13	49
19:9–10	13, 55, 128	26:34–35	43, 54, 59–62
19:30	115		
20:9	9	26:46	58, 72
21:17–23	120	27:34	58
23:22	13, 55, 128		
23:23–32	71	**NUMBERS**	
24:5–9	115–17	4:7–8	116
25	23, 42, 45, 54–55, 57, 59, 61–72	7:1	85
		10:1–10	71
		11	96
25—26	57–63, 72, 113	11:20	99
		11:31	99
25:1–7	23, 58–62	15:32–36	107

17:3–4	84	22:4	136
28:9–10	115	22:28–29	26
29:1–11	71	23:2 [1]	120
29:6	116	23:20–21 [19–20]	47
32	66	23:20 [19]	12
		24:10–11	12–13
DEUTERONOMY		24:12–13	13
3:8–22	66	24:17	13
3:20	89	24:19–21	13, 55, 128
4:1	31	26:5	20
4:25–31	31	26:12–13	13
5:6–9	73	27:16	9
5:12–15	73, 106–9,	28:36–37	31
	113	28:64–67	31
5:14	107, 134,	29:1—39:20	31
	136	32:6	18
5:15	108	32:10	82
12:2–14	31		
14:21	151	**JOSHUA**	
14:28–29	13, 55	1:13–15	89
15	5, 25, 30–31,	6:4–20	71
	35, 41–42,	12:6	66
	44–45, 53–54,	13:8	66
	59, 61, 65,	23:1	89
	68, 77, 139		
15:1–18	23–24, 30,	**JUDGES**	
	113	1:34	52
15:1–11	37–41	2:18	52
15:1–3	37, 45, 47,	3:17	85
	49, 134, 140	3:27	71
15:1	45	4:3	52
15:2–3	40	5:6–11	28
15:2	41	6:9	52
15:7–11	12–13	7:8	71
15:7	33, 40	7:16	71
15:8	40	7:18–22	71
15:9–11	54	10:12	52
15:9	40–41	16:20	49
15:12–18	31–34, 45,		
	47	**RUTH**	
15:12	26, 27	1:8	8
15:13–14	34	2	13, 55, 128
15:16	25, 32	4:1–12	18
16:9–12	13		
16:16	34	**1 SAMUEL**	
17:14–20	31	2:1–10	19
21:18–21	9	2:10	86, 128
		2:29	85

4:6	27	15:10	71
4:9	27	15:24	129
8:11–17	13–14	15:29	129
9:16	17, 50, 86	15:35	129
10:1	15, 17, 86	17:15	129
10:18	52	18:16	71
12:7	86	19:11	129
12:21	82	20:1	71
13:3	27, 71	20:22	71
13:7	26–27	20:25	129
13:19	27	22:51	86
14:11	27	23:1	86
14:21	27		
16:1	86	**1 KINGS**	
16:6	86	1:34	71
16:13	86	1:39	71, 86
20:5	116	1:41	71
20:18	116	1:45	86
20:24	116	2:26–27	129
20:27	116	2:35	129
21:1–9	128, 130	3:6–9	18
21:1–6	127	3:7	17
21:4–6	93	5:2–5	69
22:7	14	5:3	85, 89
24:6	86	5:4	89
29:3	27	5:13–18	13
		8:16	17, 128
2 SAMUEL		8:22–26	69
1:14–16	86	8:23–26	18
1:21	86	8:25	17
2:4	86	8:56	89
2:28	71	9:5	17
5:3	86	10:9	17
6:15	71	11:31–37	17
7:1–16	17	12:4–14	49
7:1–17	69	17:1–16	138
7:1	89	19:11–14	111
7:2	128		
7:5–7	128	**2 KINGS**	
7:5	18	4:23	116
7:8	18	5:1–14	138
7:11	89	9:13	71
7:14–15	18	11:5–9	116
7:19–21	18	11:12	86
7:25–29	18	13:4	52
8:17	129	13:22	52
12:20	85	16:18	116, 120

17:19–20	43
21:10–15	43
22:16–17	43
23:26–27	43
23:30	86
23:32	43
23:37	43
24:3	43
24:20	43
25	18
25:4–7	43

1 CHRONICLES

9:32	116
11:3	86
15:28	71
22:9	89
23:31	115–16
24:27	26
29:22	86
31:3	115

2 CHRONICLES

2:4	115–16
8:13	115–16
10:4–14	49
15:14	71
23:4–8	116
23:11	86
28:15	85
31:3	115–16
36:22–33	69

EZRA

1:1–3a	69
3:5	116
6:21	48
9:1—10:44	48

NEHEMIAH

4	48
4:12–14 [18–20]	71
5:1–13	46–51
5:7–9	48
5:13	49, 51, 73, 135
6	48
10	57, 77

10:29–32 [28–31]	48
10:32 [31]	63–64, 114
10:34 [33]	115–16
13:15–22	110, 114

ESTHER

1:19–20	91
8:8	91

JOB

1	11
3:8	84
6:18	82
12:24	82
22:6	13
22:9	13
22:14	84
24:3–4	13
24:9	13
24:23	13
26:7	82
29:12–17	13
31:13–23	13
34:28	50
37:18	84
38:8–11	84, 97
39:24–25	71

PSALMS

2:2	86
2:7	18
8:4	125
9:7–9	18
9:12	50
10:14–16	18
10:18	18
12:5	18
15	21
18:50	86
20:6	86
21	15
22:26–28	18
23:4–5	20
23:5–6	126
24:2	84
27:10	18
28:8	86
33:6–7	97

36:7–9	20	20:16	13
41:1–2	18	27:13	13
45	15	29:14	16
45:7	85	31:10–31	8
47:6 [5]	71		
48	15	**SONG OF SONGS**	
65:5	20	3:4	8
65:9–13	20	8:4	8
68:5	13, 19		
68:6	19	**ISAIAH**	
69:33	19	1:2–4	18
72	15, 17	1:9–17	50
72:1–4	17	1:12–17	130
72:12–14	17	1:13	110,
72:16	16–17		115–16
73:4	85	1:23	13
74:13–15	84	2:2–4	118
81:4 [3]	71, 116	5	50
82:3–4	19	5:8	14
84:9	86	6	116
89:3–37	18	9:4	49
89:20–51	86	10:27	49
94:6	13	11:1–9	16
98:6	71	14:25	49
103:6	19	18:3	71
103:13	18	19:20	52
104:5–9	84	24:10	82
107:40	82	27:13	71
109:23	49	29:21	82
112:1–3	19	33:9	49
113:7–9	19	33:15	49
128:2–3	20	34:11	82
132:15	20	40	119
132:17	86	40:12	97
136:15	49	40:17	82
140:12	18	40:19	84
146:7–10	19	40:22	84
146:9	13	40:23	82
147:6	19	41:29	82
147:8	20	42:14	18
147:14	20	43:3	18
150:3	71	43:15	18
		44:6	18
PROVERBS		44:9	82
8:27–28	84	44:24	84
9	8	45	18
14:1	8	45:1–17	15

45:1	18, 75, 86	7:6	13
45:4	18	7:12–14	128
45:18–19	82	10:9	84
47:6	49	17	44
48:17	18	17:21–27	110, 114
48:20	18	17:27	43
49:4	82	22:3	13
49:7	18	22:13–16	17
49:1–2	18	22:13–14	13
51:9	84	23:5–6	16
52:2	49	27:2–12	49
55:1–5	126	28:2	49
56—66	119	28:10–14	49
56	70, 146	30:8	49
56:1–8	117–21	31:9	18
56:7–8	70, 120	33:14–16	16
58:1	71	34	43, 46, 55
58:5–7	114	34:2–5	43
58:6	49	34:8–22	41–46
58:9	49	34:8	45
58:10–11	114	34:9	26–27, 45
58:13	110, 114	34:10–11	45
59:4	82	34:12–22	44
60	57, 75, 77	34:14	26–27, 45
60:1–3	74–76	37:5–11	44
60:17–20	74–76	39:4–7	43
61	57, 77, 124	51:27	71
61:1–6	74–76		
61:1–2	120	**LAMENTATIONS**	
61:1	75, 85	1:14	49
63:8	18	2:6	115
63:16	18	2:8	116
64:8	18	3:27	49
66:12	119	5:5	49
66:13	18, 119		
66:18	119	**EZEKIEL**	
66:23	116, 119	1—2	116
		1:22–26	84
JEREMIAH		2:1	125
3:4	18	10:1	84
3:19	18	16:9	85
4:5	71	16:49	50
4:19–21	71	18:8	12
4:23	82	18:13	12
6:1	71	18:17	12
6:17	71	22:7	13
		22:12	12

33:3–6   71
34:3   85
34:20   85
34:27   49
45:8–12   17
45:17   115–16
46:1–12   116
46:1–2   115–16
46:3   116
46:16–17   14

DANIEL
1:15   85–86
6:8   91
6:24–27   91
7:13   125
10:3   85

HOSEA
2:8–23   16
2:11   110, 115–16
5:8   71
6:6   130
8:1   71
11:1–4   18

JOEL
2:1   71

AMOS
2:2   71
2:8   13
3:1   112
3:6   71
3:9–10   112
3:13   112
3:15   112
4:1   112
4:4–5   114
5:1   112
5:7   112
5:10–12   112
5:24   21
7:1–9   110–11
7:13   114
7:14   111
7:16   112
8:1–14   110

8:1–3   111
8:4–6   112–13
8:5   110, 114–16
8:10–11   111
8:11   112
8:4–7   109–15
9:1–4   110
9:11–15   110
9:11   16
9:13–15   16
9:13   73

JONAH
1:9   26

MICAH
4:1–3   118
6:6–8   130
6:8   21

NAHUM
1:13   49

HABAKKUK
1:16   85–86
3:13   86

ZEPHANIAH
1:16   71

ZECHARIAH
7:10   13
9:14   71
11:6   85

MALACHI
1:6   18
2:10   18
3:5   13

1 MACCABEES
6   57, 77
6:48–54   64–65

MATTHEW
6   142
6:9–15   139–40
12:1–8   124
12:8   127
12:9–14   125
26:11   12

MARK

2:1–12	125
2:10	126
2:13–17	126, 129
2:18–22	126
2:21–22	127
2:23—3:6	124–33
2:23–28	126–27
2:26	128
2:27–28	125–27
3:1–6	125–27
3:2–4	136
6:13	85
8:31	125
9:12	125
11:25	139
14:7	12
14:8	85
14:21	125
14:41	125
16:1	85

LUKE

1:46–55	19
4:14	138
4:16–21	137–39
4:18	85
6:1–5	124
6:5	128
6:6–11	125
6:7–9	136
7:46	85
11:2–4	139–40
12:16–21	140–42
12:22–34	142
13:10–17	134–35
14:1–6	135–36

JOHN

9:1–41	136–37
12:3	85
12:8	12

ACTS

10:38	85

COLOSSIANS

2:16	116

HEBREWS

1:9	85